CAMBRIDGE
UNIVERSITY PRESS

ICT Starters

On Track Stage 2

Victoria Ellis, Sarah Lawrey and Doug Dickinson

CAMBRIDGE
UNIVERSITY PRESS

University Printing House, Cambridge CB2 8BS, United Kingdom

One Liberty Plaza, 20th Floor, New York, NY 10006, USA

477 Williamstown Road, Port Melbourne, VIC 3207, Australia

314–321, 3rd Floor, Plot 3, Splendor Forum, Jasola District Centre, New Delhi – 110025, India

79 Anson Road, #06–04/06, Singapore 079906

Cambridge University Press is part of the University of Cambridge.

It furthers the University's mission by disseminating knowledge in the pursuit of education, learning and research at the highest international levels of excellence.

www.cambridge.org
Information on this title: www.cambridge.org/9781108463553

First published 2003
Second edition 2005
Third edition 2013
Fourth edition 2019

20 19 18 17 16 15 14 13 12 11 10 9 8 7 6 5 4 3 2 1

Printed in the United Kingdom by Latimer Trend

A catalogue record for this publication is available from the British Library

ISBN 978-1-108-46355-3 Paperback

Additional resources for this publication at www.cambridge.org/9781108463553

Cambridge University Press has no responsibility for the persistence or accuracy of URLs for external or third-party internet websites referred to in this publication, and does not guarantee that any content on such websites is, or will remain, accurate or appropriate. Information regarding prices, travel timetables, and other factual information given in this work is correct at the time of first printing but Cambridge University Press does not guarantee the accuracy of such information thereafter.

All exam-style questions and sample answers in this title were written by the authors. In examinations, the way marks are awarded may be different.

....

Introduction

Cambridge ICT Starters: On Track Stage 2 has been written to support you in your work on the Cambridge International Diploma ICT Starters syllabus (On Track Stage 2) from 2019. This book provides full coverage of all of the modules so that you will have a good platform of skills and information to support you in the next stages of your development of ICT capability. The modules can be studied in any order.

The book supports your work on the key skills needed at this level to become knowledgeable in programming, website design, networks, as well as video and animation.

The book provides you and your helpers with:

- examples of activities to complete
- exercises to practise the skills before you put them into practice
- final projects to show just how much you have learned
- optional scenario and challenge activities for those who want to challenge themselves further.

The book has been designed for use in the classroom, with help and support from trained teachers. The tasks, skills and activities have been set in real-life situations where computer access will be essential. At the start of each module, there is a section called 'Before you start …' which explains what you need to know before you begin your work. The activities are designed to lead you towards a final project where you will have the opportunity to demonstrate your knowledge and understanding of each of the skills.

Some exercises require you to open prepared files for editing. These files are available to be downloaded by your teachers from www.cambridge.org/9781108463553. You will find that the website provides the files to get you started. These files are included to help you start the activities in this book.

The modules in this book refer to examples from Scratch 3, Notepad, Pencil 2d, Adobe Spark and Audacity. Using these will develop your digital skills and will mean that the notes and activities in the book will be easy for you to follow. However, your teacher may decide to use different applications to help you to meet the module objectives.

We hope that you will enjoy working on this stage and take pleasure in developing your ICT skills!

Good luck!

Contents

On Track Stage 2

Introduction

How to use this book

In every module, look out for these features:

Module objectives: This table shows you the key things that you will learn in this module.

	In this module you will:	Pass/Merit	Done?
1	Plan an interactive program using abstraction	P	
2	Create and test an interactive program using selection, input and output	P	

Key terms: These boxes provide you with definitions of words that may be important or useful.

> **Key term**
>
> **Router:** a component that connects computers and networks together.

Did you know?: These boxes provide interesting information and opportunities for further research.

> **Did you know?**
>
> The first website to go online was the website http://info.cern.ch. It went online on 6 August 1991.

Tip: These boxes give you handy hints as you work.

> **Tip**
>
> You could use the list of superheroes on the Encyclopaedia Britannica website.

Challenge: These activities are more difficult and extend beyond the syllabus.

Challenge

Scenario: These are tasks that help you practise everything you have learnt in the module in a "real-life" situation.

Scenario

Superheroes are awesome!

Pass/Merit: This shows you the level of all of the activities in the book.

| Skill 6 | P/M | M | P |

Skill box: These boxes contain activities for you to test what you have learnt.

Skill 1

Entering data

Watch out! box: These boxes help you to avoid making mistakes in your work.

> **WATCH OUT!**
>
> Be careful if you are taking images from the internet. Make sure that the sites you want to visit are safe.

Stay safe!: These boxes contain important e-safety advice.

> **Stay safe!**
>
> When using the internet for research, make sure that you only use trusted websites.

Programming for a purpose

	In this module you will:	Pass/Merit	Done?
1	Plan an interactive program using abstraction	P	
2	Create and test an interactive program using selection, input and output	P	
3	Predict the output of an interactive program that uses input and selection	P	
4	Create and formally test an interactive program using selection, input and output	M	
5	Correct (debug) a short interactive program containing more than one error.	M	

In this module you are going to develop skills to help you work towards your final project, which will be using Scratch to create a game where a player can look after a virtual pet. The player of your game will need to feed and play with the pet to make sure it doesn't get too hungry or bored!

You will learn how to plan, design, create and test a program before you start to make your game. Before you can start planning your game, you need to learn some new skills in Scratch. These skills will be used as part of the final game.

You will learn how to:

- use variables
- broadcast
- change the costume of a Sprite
- change the background of a game
- detect collisions
- use timers and wait
- use random numbers.

Once you have learnt what these new skills are, and how they are used, you will be able to think about them when you design your game.

Before you start

You should:

- have used Scratch to create simple programs, including sequences, repetition and procedures
- have fixed problems in your own programs to make sure they work
- have had experience of using and creating flowcharts to plan a program.

Introduction

Computer programs need to be planned and designed before they are created. This is usually done following something called the **Software Development Cycle**. This is a structured sequence of actions that allow you to plan, design, create, **test** and then improve a computer program.

It is important that programs are planned first for many reasons, such as:

- to make it clear what the program has to do
- to make sure everyone on the team working on it fully understands the requirements
- to make sure the person (or group of people) who want the game are happy with what the game will do.

From this plan, you can design how the program will work, for example using a flowchart. This will let you find any problems before you start, and it means you're not making it up as you go along!

Once you have created your program you need to test it to make sure it works fully and that there aren't any problems. If you have been asked to make a particular program for a client, they will have a clear idea of what they want. If you cannot deliver the program they want, you may not get paid for the work you have done – if it doesn't work, for example.

> **Key terms**
>
> **Software Development Cycle:** a formal set of processes followed to plan, design, create and test a system.
>
> **Test:** to make sure a section of code runs correctly.

Key terms

Interactive: a program that has both input and output for the user.

Interface: the part of a program that lets the user input data and that produces output for the user.

Input: putting data into a computer, for example typing, clicking buttons.

Output: data being given from the computer to the user, for example on screen, from speakers.

Analogue: data in the real world (that is not in a computer).

Programs usually require user **interaction** using an **interface**. The interface is the part of the program that allows the user to interact with it. It includes the on-screen buttons, text, images and so on, that the user can then click, type into and look at.

An interactive program means that the user is involved in the program and they are able to:

- put data into the computer. This is **input**, for example clicking buttons, typing text and numbers. In a computer game, this might be by using a hand-held controller.
- get data from the computer. This is **output**, for example you can see images and text, and hear sound.

Stay safe!

You might be using the 'Scratch Internet' version. Make sure you stay safe while online, and only use the website you have been given. Do not talk to other people online, or visit other websites without the permission of your teacher.

Most data that is in the real world (that is not in a computer) is **analogue** data. This can be any value, represented in any form, for example sound or images. This data must be converted for a computer to understand it.

A computer only understands **digital** data. This is 1s and 0s. If you want to input data into a computer, it has to be turned into 1s and 0s. This can be done with any type of data, for example letters, numbers, sound and images. This is **data capture**.

This image shows an analogue sound wave at the top, that can have a large range of values, and a digital wave at the bottom where the data has been encoded as 1s and 0s. The digital sound wave is not identical to the analogue sound wave.

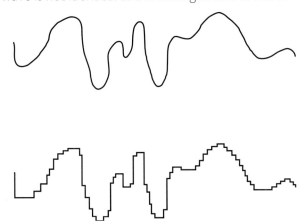

A special form of input and output is known as **feedback**. This is when the output from a process becomes the input into a process. So it is all run automatically, and the data that is created changes what happens next.

Key terms

Digital: data in a computer; it is stored in 1s and 0s.

Data capture: gathering data from the real world and turning it into a form the computer understands.

Feedback: the input changes the program, which then produces output. The output becomes the new input in the program.

Skill 1

Detecting user interaction 1: detecting click buttons

A computer game might need the user to press buttons, for example a keypress. In a car driving game, the car is going to move forward when the up arrow is clicked. The game needs to know when the up arrow has been clicked by the user so it knows when to move the car.

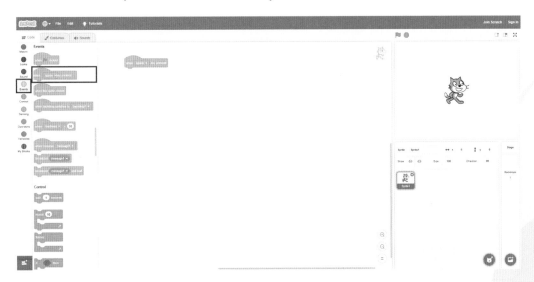

To do this in Scratch, you will need to click on **Events** and then drag

Next, you need to click on the down arrow next to the word 'space'.

You would then choose the key from the drop-down box.

You would then add instructions for when this key is pressed below this block.

Activity 1.1

Open a new Scratch window.

Right-click on the cat Sprite.

Select 'Delete'.

Click on the 'New Sprite' button.

Add a car Sprite to a new Scratch file.

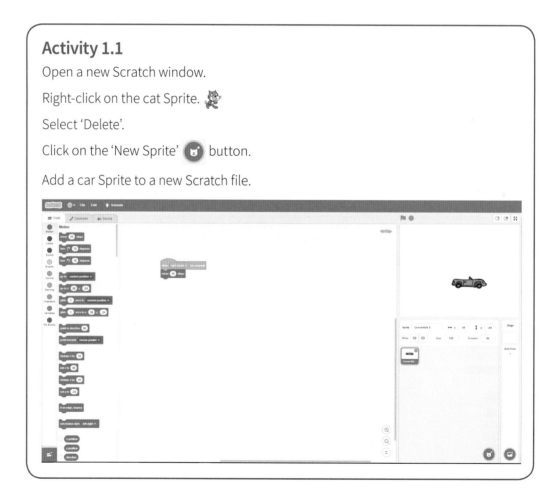

Make sure it is facing to the right of the screen.

Add blocks so when the right arrow key is pressed, the car moves ten spaces.

Test your code works.

Activity 1.2

Add new blocks so when the left arrow key is pressed the car moves back ten spaces.

Test your code works.

Activity 1.3

Add new blocks so when the up arrow key is pressed the car rotates left 90 degrees.

Test your code works.

Activity 1.4

Add new blocks so when the down arrow key is pressed the car rotates right 90 degrees.

Test your code works.

> **Tip**
>
> Moving back will have a negative number, for example –10.

Skill 2

Detecting user interaction 2: user clicking objects

You can get your user to interact with your game by clicking on objects in the actual game, for example when the user clicks on the car, the car moves forward.

Start by clicking on the Sprite.

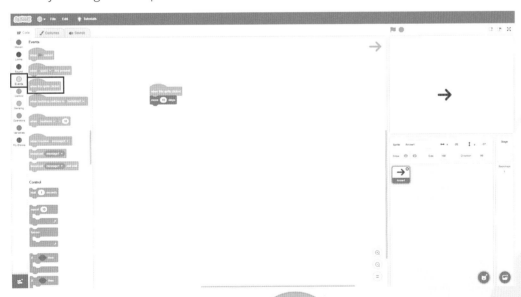

Then you can click on **Events** and then drag `when this sprite clicked` .

Finally, you can add your instructions for when this Sprite is clicked below this block.

Activity 2.1

Add a Sprite to a new Scratch program.

When the Sprite is clicked make the Sprite move forward.

Test your code works.

Activity 2.2

Change the program from **Activity 2.1**. When the Sprite is clicked, make the Sprite:

1 Move forward 20 steps
2 Turn left 90 degrees
3 Move forward 20 steps
4 Turn right 90 degrees
5 Move forward 20 steps

Test your code works.

Tip

To slow your Sprite down so you can see it move, add a 'Wait' block after each instruction.

Skill 3

Broadcasting: make a car move when you click on a Sprite

When you add code to a Sprite, you can affect only that Sprite.

Broadcasting lets you send out a message to tell another Sprite to do something, for example move.

This is how to make a car move ten steps when the ball is clicked.

First, you need to add a car Sprite and a ball Sprite to your Scratch stage.

Key term

Broadcast: sending a message in Scratch that other Sprites can see, and then react to.

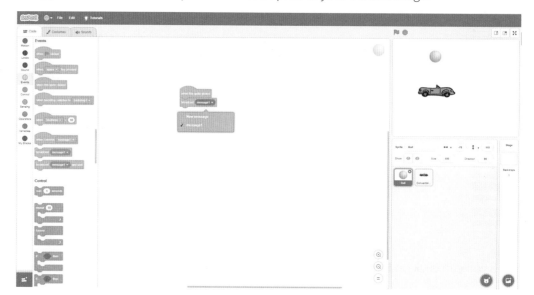

For the ball Sprite

Next, you need to click on **Events** and then drag  and also drag

 .

You would then click on the drop-down menu and choose 'New Message'.

You will need to change the message to make it meaningful. It should describe its purpose, for example Car Move.

For the car Sprite

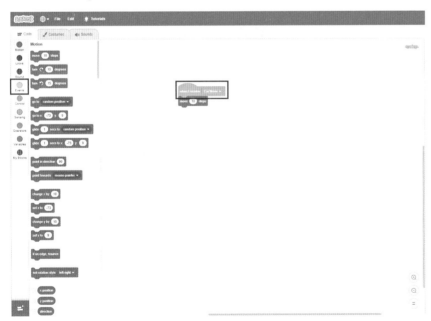

You would start by clicking on **Events**.

You would then drag  .

Next, you need to choose the correct broadcast message from the drop-down menu. You can then add your action blocks below it.

Activity 3.1

Open a new Scratch window.

Add two car Sprites.

When the first car is clicked, make the second car move forward.

When the second car is clicked, make the first car move forward.

Test your code works.

Activity 3.2

Open a new Scratch window.

Add a dinosaur Sprite.

Add four other Sprites, one to move the dinosaur forward, one for moving back, one for turning left, one for turning right.

Add blocks so that when moving forward is clicked it broadcasts a message. When the dinosaur receives this message it moves forward. Repeat for moving back, and turning left and right.

Test your code works.

Skill 4

Variables

A **variable** allows you to store data in a program, for example a number. This data is stored in the computer's memory, a bit like putting something in a box. You give the variable a name so you can remember what it is called, and use it later. You might have lots of variables, so they all need to have names that describe what they are storing.

In a game where you are catching stars, you might want to count how many stars have been caught. This would be stored in a variable; it could be named Stars.

In a game where your spaceship is flying through space, you might want to store the number of planets it has visited. This would be stored in a variable; it could be named Planets.

This variable is called Points. At the moment there is the number 0 in the Points box.

Points
0

You can change the value in Points. For example, you could change Points to the number 2.

The variable now has 2 stored in it.

Points
2

You could ask the variable what is in it. If you asked Points what is in it, it would tell you '2'.

You can add to the value in Points. For example, you could add 1 to the current value.

Points currently has 2 in it, so 2 + 1 = 3.

The variable now has 3 stored in it.

Points
3

You could add 10 to it.

Points currently has 3 in it, so 3 + 10 = 13.

The variable now has 13 stored in it.

Points
13

Now you could subtract 3 from it.
Points currently has 13 in it, so 13 – 3 = 10.

The variable now has 10 stored in it.

Points
10

If you asked Points what it has in it now, what would it say? 10.

Creating a variable

1 To create a variable, first you need to click on **Variables**.

2 Then you would click on 'Make a Variable'.

3 You should give the variable a meaningful name. You will need to remember what it is called later.

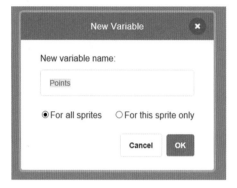

Tip

You are probably only going to need to use 'For all Sprites'.

'For all Sprites' means any Sprite can change and read the variable.

'For this Sprite only' means that this Sprite only can change and read the variable.

4 Next, you would click 'OK'.

The new variable called Points will appear on the screen.

If you don't want to see what the value is, you can untick the box on the left of the word 'Points'.

Setting a variable

You can set the value of a variable by dragging .

You then enter the number you want the variable to start at in the box.

To set the variable to a starting value (for example 0 when the program starts), put a 'When green flag clicked' block followed by the 'set Points to 0' block.

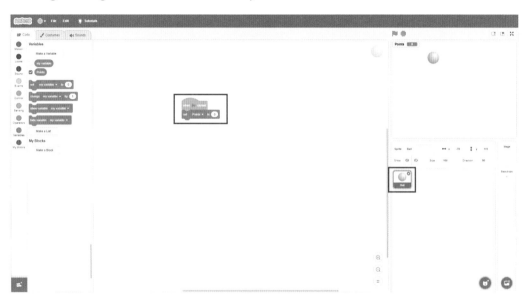

Changing a variable

You can change the value of a variable by dragging .

You will then enter the number you want to change the value by; 1 means increase it by 1.

2 would increase it by 2.
−5 would decrease it by 5.

In this example, whenever the ball Sprite is clicked, the variable is increased by 1.

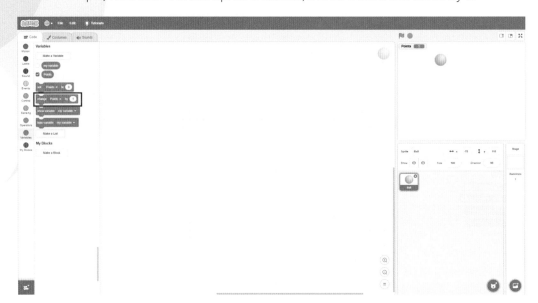

Activity 4.1

Open a new Scratch window.

Create a variable with the name Count. Set it 'For all Sprites'.

Each time the Sprite is clicked, increase the variable by 1.

Activity 4.2

Add a second Sprite to your program.

When this Sprite is clicked, increase the variable by 5.

Activity 4.3

Add a third Sprite to your program.

When this Sprite is clicked, decrease the variable by 2.

Test your code works each time.

Skill 5

Selection

Selection is when you use a question to decide what to do.

The most common selection is the 'if' statement. This only has two possible answers: Yes and No.

An example would be "Should I finish all my homework?". The choices are: Yes or No. If you choose Yes then you do your homework. If you choose No, then you don't.

You can use this with a variable. For example if the number of points is equal to 10, make the Sprite say "You win".

Selection blocks in Scratch are in the **Control** menu.

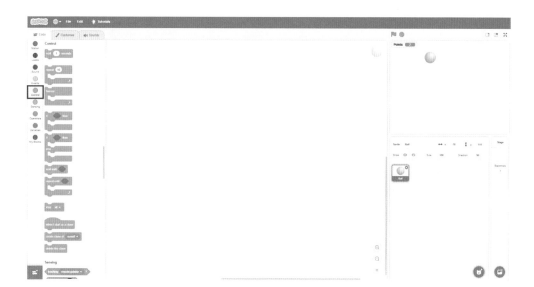

There are two options:

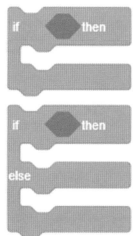

Key term

Selection: When a section of code is run depending on a condition.

Did you know?

You have to make lots of choices every day. If you decide to eat a cookie then there will be one less cookie to eat later on.

If you set the alarm, you will wake up on time (unless you hit the snooze button!). If you don't set the alarm, you will be late for school!

If 'then'

When the answer is True, then Scratch runs the commands inside the block. If the answer is False, the code is not run, for example:

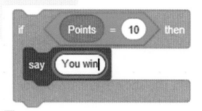

If the value in Points is equal to 10, then it will output 'You win'. If it is not, then nothing will happen.

If 'Then Else'

When the answer is True, the statement after 'then' is run. When the answer is False, the statement after 'else' is run.

e.g.

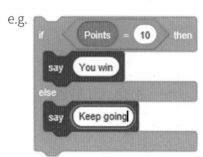

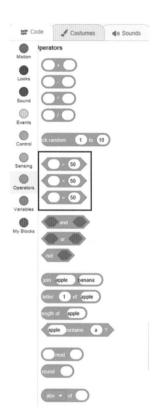

When the value in Points is equal to 10 then the output is 'You win'.

When the value in Points is not equal to 10, the output is 'Keep going'.

Creating the Selection statement

The first block needs to be an **operator**. It can be either '<', '=' or '>'.

= checks if the value on the left and the right are the same, for example:

- Is 10 = 2? False, 10 is not the same as 2.
- Is 5 > 2? True, 5 is greater than 2.
- Is 10 < 10? False, 10 is not less than 10.

The operator has a space on both sides of it. You can enter a number in a box, or put a variable in it.

Numbers are typed in the boxes.

Key term

Operator: A command that goes between two values or variables, e.g. < or >.

To add a variable, click on **Variables**, then drag the variable name into the box.

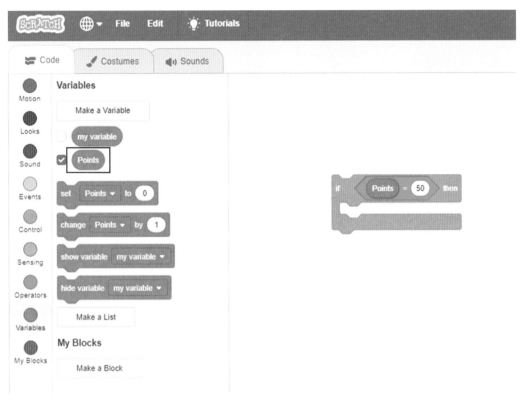

Drag the actions you want into the space under the 'if' block.

Put the 'if' under a block to tell it when to run, for example:

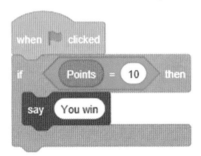

Selection with repetition

You might need to continually check a value, for example as soon as the variable 'Points' is 10 then you want to output 'You win'. If this is not inside a loop then the blocks will run once when the program first starts and never again.

Putting the 'if' block inside a 'forever' block means it will keep checking the value of the variable.

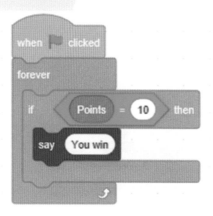

Activity 5.1

Edit the program you made for **Activity 4.3**.

Add a selection statement that constantly checks the value of your variable.

If the value is equal to 20 then output a winning message.

Activity 5.2

Edit the program. Change the selection statement. Instead of checking if the value is equal to 20, check if the value is greater than 20.

Activity 5.3

Open a new Scratch window.

Create a program that:

- When the user presses the right arrow, the Sprite moves to the right, and 1 is added to a variable.
- When the user presses the left arrow, the Sprite moves to the left, and 1 is subtracted from a variable.
- If the variable is greater than 10, a message is output.
- If the variable is less than 1, a different message is output.

Tip

\> is greater than

< is less than

10 > 2 is true

Tip

You could use two 'if' blocks. Or one 'if then else' block.

Skill 6

Collisions

In Scratch you can detect when one Sprite touches another Sprite, or another colour. You can then perform an action, for example if a car hits a star then it has a point added. When a car goes off the road then it stops.

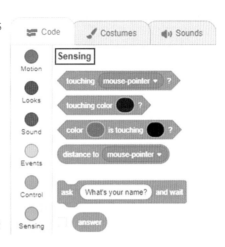

A collision can be added to a selection statement. If a collision is detected, then an action happens.

Touching a colour

To detect if a Sprite has touched a specific colour you will need to select 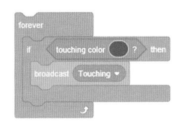 from the **Sensing** menu.

This block goes into an 'if' statement. If the Sprite is touching the colour red, then it will broadcast the message 'Touching'.

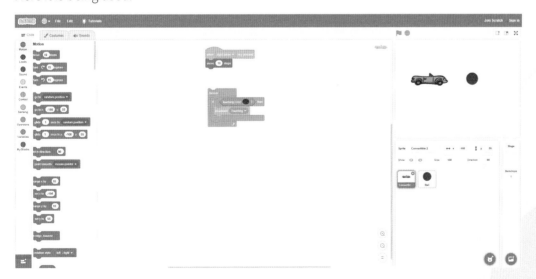

Putting this inside a 'forever' loop will keep it checking continually.

Here it is being used.

> **Tip**
>
> Another Sprite might use this message to perform another task.

The car will move when you press the right arrow key.

When it touches the red circle the message 'Touching' will be broadcast.

To create your own Sprite (like the red circle) click on the paintbrush icon.

Use the drawing tools to draw your Sprite.

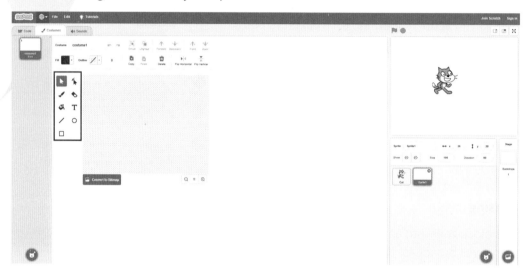

Touching another Sprite

You can also detect whether it is touching another Sprite.

To do this, from the **Sensing** menu you would choose the block touching mouse-pointer ?.

Then you would choose the Sprite from the drop-down menu.

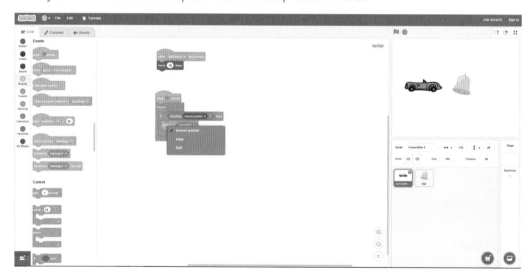

In this example, when the car touches the bell it will broadcast a message.

Activity 6.1

Create a new Scratch program.

Add one dinosaur Sprite.

Add blocks so the dinosaur can move up, down, left and right when the user clicks the arrow keys.

Add a red rectangle.

If the dinosaur touches the red shape, make it say a message.

Activity 6.2

Add a green circle to the same program.

If the dinosaur touches the green shape, make it say a different message.

Activity 6.3

Add more red and green shapes. You should not need to add any more touching commands. The dinosaur should say the same messages each time it touches a colour.

Activity 6.4

Add an insect Sprite.

Create a variable called 'Insects'. Revisit **Skill 4** to see how to create a variable.

Each time the dinosaur touches the insect Sprite, add 1 to the variable 'Insects'.

Activity 6.5

When the dinosaur touches the insect Sprite, make the insect Sprite disappear.

In the menu **Looks** the block will make the Sprite disappear. 'Show' will make the Sprite appear.

Activity 6.6

Add more insect Sprites.

Each time the dinosaur touches any of the insect Sprites, add 1 to the variable 'Insects' and make the insect disappear.

Activity 6.7

Each time the dinosaur touches any of the insect Sprites make the dinosaur say, "Yum, I like eating insects".

Tip

Use the 'touching color' block.

Tip

The 'say' block is in the **Looks** menu.

Tip

Use the 'touching color' block.

Entering data

Your user can enter data into
Scratch. You could then use
this to perform specific tasks,
for example you could give a
character a name or you could
say how many times you want to
play a game.

Getting data

The block Ask and wait is found in
the **Sensing** menu.

This code will output the
message "What's your name?"
and wait for the user to type something.

The data the user types will just
disappear. If you want, or need,
to keep it then you can store
it in a variable. In the **Sensing**
menu is the block 'answer'.

Store this in a variable directly
beneath the ask command.
You will need to change the
name of the variable you
store it in to make sure it is
appropriate. Click on the
down arrows and enter the
name you want.

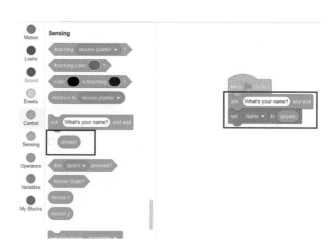

You can then use the answer elsewhere, for example here the name entered is input:

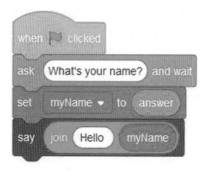

Skill 8

Validating data

You can **validate** data to check whether it is reasonable. For example if you are entering the age of the user, then an age of 239 would be unreasonable.

You do this using a selection statement, exactly the same as in **Skill 5**.

> **Key term**
>
> **Validate:** To check that data entered is reasonable, or within set limits or bounds.

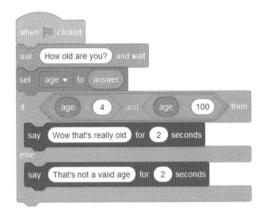

In this example the selection has been used to check whether the age is greater than 4 and less than 100.

If the age is not valid (it is not within these bounds) then it outputs "That's not a valid age".

You can make this validation even more useful by putting it within an iteration (or loop).

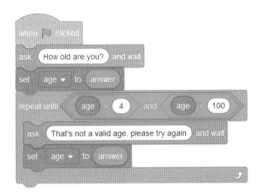

This time the validation takes place inside the repeat until. The loop will keep on saying "That's not a valid age, please try again" and taking the age as input until that age is greater than 4 and less than 100.

You can also do validation on text, for example to make sure they have entered Yes or No to answer a question.

In this example, the program will repeatedly ask "Are you ready to start?" until the user enters either "Yes" or "Y" or "y" or "yes". All four options are given because any of these are allowed to be entered.

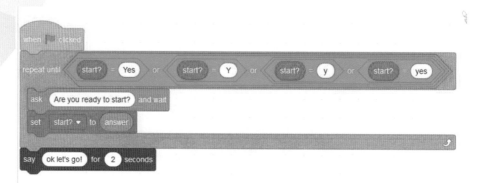

If anything else is entered it will just ask the same question again.

Activity 8.1

Create a new Scratch program.

Make the sprite ask the user a number of questions with multiple choice options. Repeatedly ask the question until the user enters one of the possible answers.

Activity 8.2

Create a Scratch program that can make three set movements.

Ask the user which movement they would like. Validate the input and keep on asking them until they give a valid choice. Then perform the movement they have selected.

Activity 8.3

Create a Scratch program where the user has to enter information about themselves e.g. their age, height, favourite colour.

Validate the inputs and output appropriate messages if the inputs are valid, and invalid.

Skill 9

Costumes

A Sprite can have several different costumes (images) that they can change between. For example you might want a character to change colour or point in a different direction.

Adding a new costume

To add a new costume, you would click on a Sprite and then choose **Costumes**.

You can either load a pre-existing Sprite, draw a new sprite, upload from a file, or take a photo.

You can edit your Sprite using the tools on the **Costumes** page.

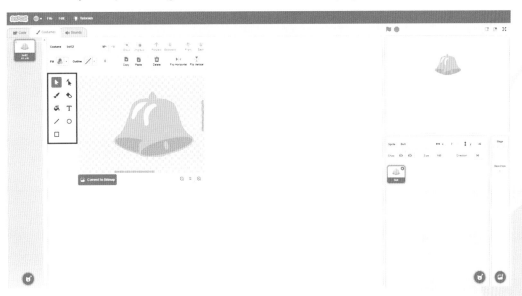

Changing costumes

The **Looks** menu lets you change costume.

You can change to a specific costume, or you can move to the next costume. The next costume will move to the next in your sequence. For example if the first costume is currently being used, then the second one will load.

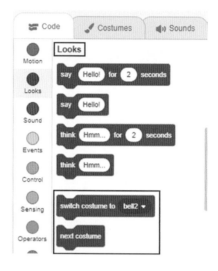

Tip

You will need a 'forever' loop and 'next costume' block.

Activity 9.1

Create a new Scratch program. Add a Sprite.

Add a second costume for the Sprite.

Add blocks so when the code runs, the Sprite keeps changing from one costume to the next.

Activity 9.2

Create a Scratch program with one Sprite that has two costumes.

Add blocks so when the right arrow key is pressed, the Sprite moves forward and changes costume.

Activity 9.3

Create a Scratch program with one Sprite that has four costumes: one for each direction the Sprite is facing (up, down, left and right).

Add blocks so when the right arrow is pressed, the Sprite loads the costume that is facing to the right.

When the up arrow is pressed, the Sprite faces up, and so on.

Activity 9.4

Create a Scratch program with a wardrobe of outfits. The user has to enter the number of the outfit they want the Sprite to wear.

Skill 10

Working with time

There are two ways you can work with time in Scratch, using the timer and using 'wait'.

The timer

Scratch has a timer built into it that you can use to time events, for example after 10 seconds you might want a new Sprite to appear.

The timer starts running as soon as the program starts.

You can then check what the time is (in seconds) by using an 'if' statement, for example 'If timer > 5 then . . .'

The timer blocks are in the **Sensing** menu.

The ⬤ timer block gets the current time (in seconds). If you tick the box then the value of the timer will appear on the screen.

The reset timer block tells the timer to go back to 0 and start again.

This Sprite program continually checks the value of the timer. If the timer is over 5 then it hides the Sprite.

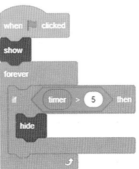

Using 'wait'

There is only one timer, so if you want lots of different things to happen at different times, and you keep resetting the timer, then it can become very complicated.

You can combine a timer with 'wait'. A 'wait' block pauses that sequence of code for the number of seconds entered, and then it continues.

The 'wait' block is in the **Control** menu.

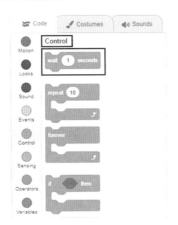

To set the number of seconds you want the sequence to pause for, you need to drag the `wait 1 seconds` block and enter the number of seconds. It will only stop that section of code.

Activity 10.1

Create a new Scratch program.

Add a Sprite with two costumes.

Add blocks so that after 5 seconds the Sprite changes costume, then after 10 seconds it changes back to the first costume.

Activity 10.2

Add a second Sprite.

After 10 seconds, make this Sprite move across the screen.

Activity 10.3

Add a variable called 'Points'.

Every 2 seconds, add 1 to the value of Points.

Add a Sprite. When the user clicks the Sprite, reset Points to 0.

Activity 10.4

Create a program that tells a short story. Set each part of the story to run based on the timer, for example a new Sprite appears at a set time.

Skill 11

Planning a program

Before you start creating your own program, you need to plan it. You can do this by using abstraction. Abstraction is where you take a real-world problem and turn it into a plan that can be created by a computer system. You can do this by identifying the inputs, outputs and processing that the program needs to do.

Inputs: this is a list of what the user will put into the program. They might be entering data, or clicking buttons. For example:

- User clicks the up arrow on the keyboard
- User clicks on the **Start** button

Outputs: this is a list of what the system will produce. It could be words and numbers that are displayed, or an image. For example:

- The background shows fields and two trees
- There is an image of a horse

- Welcome message
- Winning message

Processes: these are the actions that take place. It could be a mathematical calculation or it could be the movement of an image. For example:

- Horse moves to the right when the right arrow is pressed
- Horse changes appearance when each button is pressed
- When the horse reaches the 'Winning' circle, the winning message is displayed

Flowchart: Once you have your abstraction plan, you need to create a flowchart. You should already know how to create a flowchart, but you need to decide how many flowcharts you will have. Your game might have several procedures.

Flowchart symbols:

A flowchart starts with 'Start' and ends with 'Stop'.

A process is any action, for example mathematical functions, changing coordinates, setting a variable, changing a variable, waiting a set number of seconds. | Process |

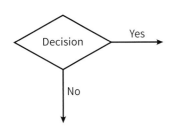

Decision is a question that has two answers, Yes and No. This works as a selection statement, for example: 'Is Point > 10?' This has a Yes and a No option.

Decision is also used to represent repetition, for example 'Has this run six times?' If No, then the loop will go back to where the repetition starts.

Button game

You will need to create a plan and design for a button game. The game has nine buttons that are all the same colour.

The aim of the game is to get all the buttons to be one colour, for example turn them from black to purple.

When the user clicks on one of the buttons it changes the colour of one or more other buttons, for example clicking Button 1 might change Button 3 to purple and Button 2 to blue.

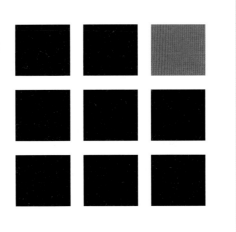

Activity 11.1

Identify the inputs for the game.

Think about the following:

1. What will the user need to do to play the game?
2. What will they click? Or enter?

Activity 11.2

Identify the outputs you need in the game.

Think about the following:

1. Are there any messages that need to be output?
2. Are there any images that need to be displayed?
3. Do any colours need to change?

Activity 11.3

Identify the processes you need in the game.

Think about the following:

1. Will anything need to move?
2. Will anything need to change?

Activity 11.4

You need to create one, or more, flowcharts for the game.

Look at your processes from **Activity 9.3** and decide if these should be procedures.

Write down each part of the game that should be its own procedure.

Activity 11.5

Draw a flowchart for each of the procedures you identified in **Activity 9.4**.

Activity 11.6

'Hit the Dragon' is a game where the user has to click on the dragons that appear on the screen. The dragons appear in different places, for different amounts of time. The player has 30 seconds to hit as many dragons as they can.

Create a plan for the game, identifying the inputs, processes and outputs.

Draw flowcharts to design how the game will work.

> **Tip**
>
> Each button is an individual element that performs its own task.

> **Tip**
>
> You should have one flowchart for each button.

> **Tip**
>
> You will need to create lots of dragon Sprites. They won't need to move. Each dragon appears at a set time, and disappears at a set time. Each time the player clicks a dragon they get a point! You will need variables and timers in this game.

Skill 12

Predicting the outcome

When you create a program, or part of a program, you should **dry-run** it to see if it will work. This involves predicting what the program will do. If you run it through and it doesn't give the correct outcome, then you know it probably won't work.

To dry-run a program, you need to perform each of the commands, by pretending you are the computer.

Look at this Scratch program: there are two Sprites: the cat and balloon.

Key term

Dry-run: follow a piece of code without using a computer. Read each line and do what it says to see if it works.

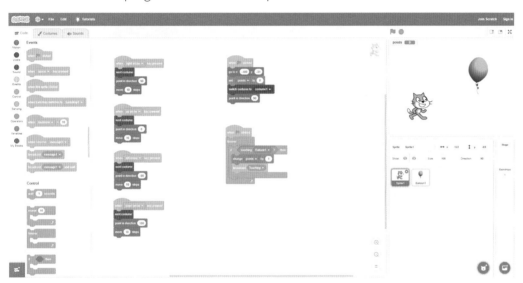

The blocks shown are for the cat.

There is a new block here:

Block	Description
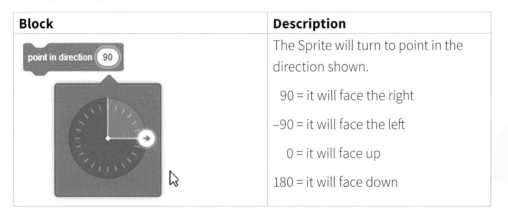	The Sprite will turn to point in the direction shown. 90 = it will face the right −90 = it will face the left 0 = it will face up 180 = it will face down

1 What will happen when the up arrow is pressed? Find the code that runs when the up arrow is pressed.

Read each line of code pretending to be the computer. What will happen?

- The cat will change to the next costume.
- It will point up (direction 0) and it will move 10 steps.

2 What will happen when the game starts, in other words when the green flag is clicked? Find the code that runs when the up arrow is pressed.

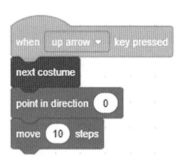

There are two procedures that run here.

Procedure 1:

- The cat will move to coordinates –100, –31.
- It will change to Costume1.
- It will point to the right (direction 90).
- It will change the value of the variable Points to 0.

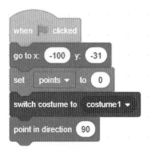

Procedure 2:

- It will keep checking if the cat is touching the Sprite Balloon1.
- If it is touching it, it will increase the value of the variable Points to 1 . . .
- . . . and it will broadcast the message 'Touching'.

Here's the code for the balloon Sprite:

You can predict what will happen when the cat touches the balloon.

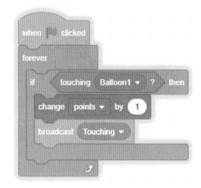

- The balloon will turn right 90 degrees and move forward 100 steps.

All of the following activities will use this next program.

Tip

You already know from the previous prediction that the message 'Touching' will be broadcast. So what happens when the balloon receives 'Touching'?

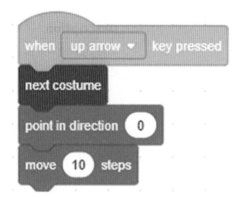

Parrot Hunt

A Scratch program called Parrot Hunt has nine Sprites – one parrot and eight stars. The user has to move the parrot around the screen collecting the stars. The stars give the parrot points, each star might give a different number of points. The user wins by getting more than 50 points. When the parrot hits a star, that star disappears for a set time.

These are the Sprites in the game:

This is the code for the parrot Sprite.

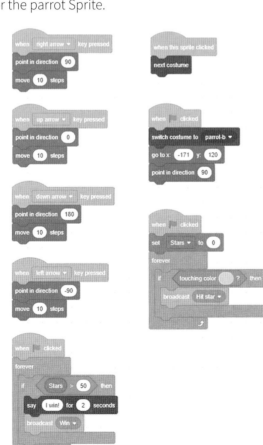

There is a new block here:

Block	Description
	The Sprite will move to the coordinates given: • x is the horizontal position • y is the vertical position. The larger the x number, the further to the right of the screen it is. The larger the y number, the further to the top of the screen it is.

The table gives the code for each Sprite.

Star number	Code
1	when I receive Hit star change Stars by 1 hide wait 4 seconds show when clicked show when I receive Win hide
2	when I receive Hit star change Stars by 1 hide wait 2 seconds show when I receive Win hide when clicked show
3	when I receive Hit star change Stars by 3 hide wait 10 seconds show when I receive Win hide when clicked show

Star number	Code
4	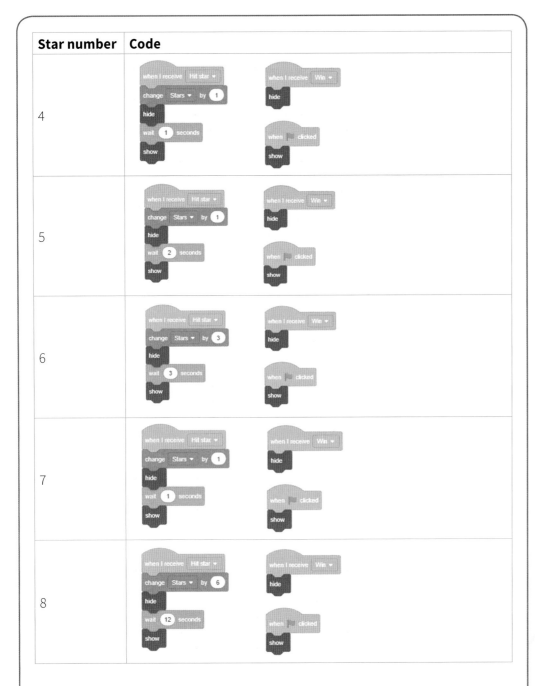
5	
6	
7	
8	

Activity 12.1

Predict what will happen when the down arrow is pressed.

Activity 12.2

Predict what will happen when the user clicks the parrot Sprite.

Activity 12.3

Predict what will happen when the parrot touches Star 6.

Activity 12.4
Predict what will happen when the green flag is clicked.

Activity 12.5
Predict what will happen when the value of the variable Stars reaches 51.

Skill 13

Testing the program

When you have created a program you need to test it to prove that it works.

A program should be tested with:

- **Normal data:** this is what you expect to be entered and should be allowed.
- **Extreme data:** this is allowed but at the edge of what is allowed.
- **Erroneous data:** this is invalid, or incorrect data, that should not be allowed.

For example if you have a program that asks you to enter your age:

Test data	Test data type
15	Normal
100	Extreme
2222	Erroneous

Not all programs can be tested with all three types of data. For example if a program only works on up, down, left and right key presses then you couldn't do any extreme tests.

A story game has a number of mathematical questions that a user has to get right to continue through the game. The game can only be played by people aged between 10 and 16, so the player has to enter their age to start. In one of these puzzles, to open a chest the player needs to work out what 15 * 4 is and enter it.

Here's a test table for the game:

Item being tested	Input	Expected result	Did it work?
User entering age	13	Accepted	
User entering age	10	Accepted	
User entering age	16	Accepted	
User entering age	9	Too young	
User entering age	17	Too old	
Chest puzzle	60	Correct	
Chest puzzle	59	Incorrect answer	
Chest puzzle	61	Incorrect answer	
Chest puzzle	30	Incorrect answer	

To test your program you will need a test table. In this you write down all the tests you are going to perform, and what you expect to happen.

Here's a test table for the Parrot Hunt game:

Item being tested	Input	Expected result	Did it work?
Up arrow pressed	Up arrow on keyboard	• Character moves up	
Down arrow pressed	Down arrow on keyboard	• Character moves down	
Parrot moves its wings when clicked	Click on parrot with mouse	• Parrot moves its wings	
Parrot touches Star 1	Move parrot until it touches Star 1	• Stars variable increases by 1 • Star 1 disappears • Star 1 reappears after 2 seconds	
Parrot touches Star 2	Move parrot until it touches Star 2	• Stars variable increases by 1 • Star 2 disappears • Star 2 reappears after 4 seconds	
Stars variable goes over 50	Move parrot until it collects enough Stars to get more than 50 points	• Parrot says "I win" • All stars disappear	

When designing a test table you need to make sure every part of your game is tested to make sure it works.

When you have created your test table, you need to actually test your program! Carry out each of the actions you said you would, and compare what happened to what you said would happen. Did it work?

If it did work – that's great, then you will write that it did in the table.

If it didn't work – that's ok. You can write that it didn't work, then look at your program and debug it (see **Skill 12**). Then test it again! Keep doing this until everything is working.

Activity 13.1

Look at the Parrot Hunt game from **Activity 10**. There are more tests that can be carried out than are given in this example table.

Create a test table and add tests that are missing from those given.

Activity 13.2

Create a test table for the dinosaur game you created in **Activity 6**.

Carry out all your tests.

Complete the test table. Did they work?

Activity 13.3

Create a test table for **Activity 7.2** where the user enters how far the Sprite moves and turns.

Activity 13.4

Create a test table for the changing costumes program you created in **Activity 7.3**.

Carry out all your tests.

Complete the test table. Did they work?

Activity 13.5

Create a test table for the story you created in **Activity 9.4**.

Carry out all your tests.

Complete the test table. Did they work?

Activity 13.6

Swap computers with a friend and test each other's games. Did they work?

Skill 14

Debugging the program

At some point your program will not do exactly what you want it to do. This might be at the end, when you use your test table, or it might be part way through. It's ok for things to go wrong! No one gets everything right first time (even the experts).

The only thing that matters is that you find out why and where it went wrong so you can fix it. Finding the error is called **debugging**.

> **Key term**
>
> **Debug:** to find errors in a program so they can be fixed.

There are lots of ways you can debug your program; two of these are:

- Dry-run your program yourself and work out what each step will do (see **Skill 10**). By checking each stage you can work out where it doesn't do what it is supposed to do.
- Read your program to a friend. Tell them what your program should do, and then work through each step with them to find out where it goes wrong.

It's always useful to keep a record of what has gone wrong and how you have fixed it. You can do this by creating a document that shows the changes (that is, you write down what went wrong).

Feeding the dragon

The dragon program has the following Sprites. One of the fish is currently invisible.

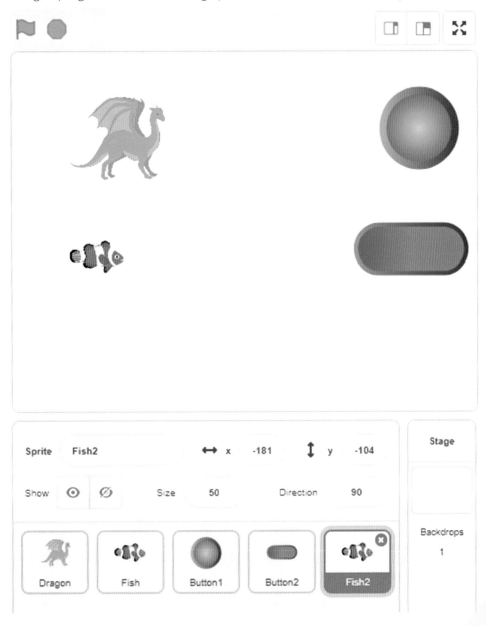

Activity 14.1

The game should perform the following actions:

- When the up arrow is pressed the dragon moves up
- When the down arrow is pressed the dragon moves down

- When the right arrow is pressed the dragon moves right
- When the left arrow is pressed the dragon moves left

There are two new blocks here:

Block	Description
change x by 10	The x coordinate will increase by the number in the box: x is the horizontal position. If x is positive, for example 10, then the Sprite will move to the right. If x is negative, for example –10, then the Sprite will move to the left.
change y by 10	The y coordinate will increase by the number in the box: y is the vertical position. If y is positive, for example 10, then the Sprite will move up. If y is negative, for example –10, then the Sprite will move down.

The program has an error.

Debug the code by dry-running it.

Where is the error?

_____

Activity 14.2

The game should perform the following actions:

- When the green button is clicked, the dragon should grow (increase in size).
- When the red button is clicked, the dragon should shrink (decrease in size).

This is the green button code.

This is the red button code.

This is the dragon code.

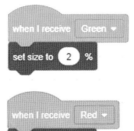

There is a new block here:

Block	Description
set size to 25 %	This will change the size of the Sprite. 100% is the normal size. A value of 50% will halve the size of the Sprite.
	A value of 200% will double the size of the Sprite.

The program has an error.

Debug the code by dry-running it.

Where is the error?

_____

Activity 14.3

When the dragon eats the fish, the Food variable increases.

When the game starts, the value in Food should be 0. So, if the game is restarted it goes back to 0.

This is the full dragon code:

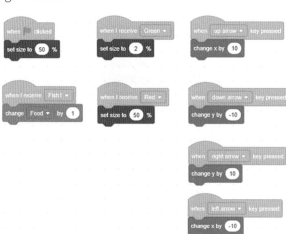

This is the code for Fish 1:

<table>
</table>

Tip

A new block is used here called 'glide'. The glide block will move the Sprite to the coordinates entered in the block. It will make the Sprite move smoothly and take the number of seconds you have entered to do this, e.g. if you have put 2 then it will take 2 seconds to move to the location.

This is the code for Fish 2:

```
when I receive  Fish1 ▾
show
forever
    go to x:  -215  y:  -98
    glide  1  secs to x:  -118  y:  19
    glide  1  secs to x:  -31  y:  -144
    glide  1  secs to x:  145  y:  -40
    glide  1  secs to x:  201  y:  -105
```

```
when  ⚑  clicked
hide
```

```
when  ⚑  clicked
forever
    if  touching  Dragon ▾  ?  then
        hide
    change  Food ▾  by  2
    broadcast  Fish1 ▾
```

Debug the code by dry-running it.

The code has two errors, can you find them both?

Scenario

Maze game

You have been asked to create a maze game.

- The user controls a character that can move through the maze.
- The character starts in a box labelled Start.
- The user has to get to a box that is labelled Finish.
- If the character touches the side of the maze then the character moves back to the start.
- There need to be some challenges along the way, for example obstacles that move which the character needs to try and avoid.
- The game keeps track of the number of times the character has to go back to the start.
- When the character reaches specific parts of the game they have to answer a question correctly before they are allowed to move again.

Activity 1

Create a plan for the game using abstraction to remove unnecessary details.

Create a list of the inputs, outputs and processes in the game.

Create a flowchart for all parts of the game.

Activity 2

Create your game using your plan.

Activity 3

Keep a record of any errors you found and how you fixed them.

Activity 4

Create a test plan for your game.

Make sure you use normal, extreme and erroneous tests (where appropriate).

Activity 5

Test your game using your test plan.

If you find any problems, debug them, and re-test them to prove it now works.

Challenge 1

You can change the background of a Scratch game.

Click on the Stage and then you can:

- choose a pre-existing background
- draw a new background
- load a background from a file
- take a photo for the background.

You can edit a background in the same way as a Sprite.

You can also create lots of different backgrounds and add code to change between them.

In the **Looks** menu you can choose 'switch backdrop', then choose the background you want from the drop-down menu.

Activity 1

Create a program that has a background from the library. Edit the background, for example change the colours.

Activity 2

Add a second background. Change the program and add a 'next level' button.

When the 'next level' button is clicked, change the background to the second background.

Challenge 2

Random numbers are very important in computer programs. These are numbers that are randomly selected by the computer. You can then use the number generated to decide what to do.

Think about random numbers like a dice.

Roll a dice:

If the number is 1, then clap your hands.

If the number is 2, then jump up and down.

If the number is 3, then sit on the floor.

If the number is 4, then sing a song.

If the number is 5, put your hands on your head.

If the number is 6, sit on your hands.

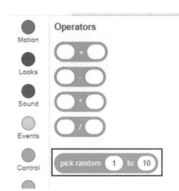

You can program a computer the same way, for example:

- In a game, the weather could be randomly generated. If the number is 1 it might rain, if it's 2 it might snow, and so on.
- A character controlled by the computer could move randomly. The computer could generate the number of steps to move each turn.

In the **Operators** menu there is a 'pick random' block.

The two numbers can be changed to anything you want! If the numbers are 1 and 10, then any number between these can be generated:

1, 2, 3, 4, 5, 6, 7, 8, 9 or 10

This block can then be used in other statements, for example it can be assigned to a variable, or used in an 'if' statement.

In this code, the variable 'Value' is given a random number between 1 and 3.

This number is then used in an 'if' statement.

If the random number is 1, the x coordinate is increased by 10.

If the random number is 2, the x coordinate is increased by 20.

If it is not 1 or 2 (i.e. it has to be 3!) then the y coordinate is increased by 10.

You need to make sure you have an 'if' for every possibility!

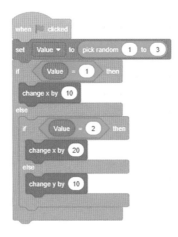

Activity 1

Create a program that generates a random number between 1 and 2.

Change the x coordinate of a Sprite by whatever the random number is.

Activity 2

Create a second Sprite. Generate two random numbers between 0 and 100.

Change the position of the Sprite to those coordinates (the first number is x, the second is y).

Activity 3

Create a program with a Sprite. Make the Sprite appear, then wait a random number of seconds before making it hide. Then wait a random number of seconds before making it appear again. Do this continually.

Final project – Virtual pet game

You have been asked to create a virtual pet game.

The game has an animal that the player needs to take care of.

The pet has a hunger value that increases every second:

- The user can set the hunger back to 0 by clicking a feed button.
- The user has to enter how much food to give the pet between 1 and 10. The number must be less than they are currently hungry because it cannot become negative.
- If the pet gets too hungry then it dies.

> **Tip**
>
> This is a large program, so you might find it easier to tackle it one small part at a time, for example just plan the first bullet point (the user can set the hunger back to 0 by clicking a feed button). Work through the activities below but only for this task.
>
> Then look at bullet 2 (if the pet gets too hungry then it dies). Work through the activities below but only for this task.
>
> Continue this way through the whole program.

The pet has a bored value that increases every few seconds:

- The user can set the bored value back to 0 by clicking a play button. The pet then plays with a ball. The pet has to ask the user a question as part of the game, which the user has to enter correctly to continue.
- If the pet gets too bored then it runs away.

The pet has an intelligence value:

- The user can increase the intelligence by clicking a train button.
- The intelligence cannot go beyond 100.

Activity 1

Create a plan for the game using abstraction to only use the key elements required.

Create a list of the inputs, outputs and processes in the game.

Create a flowchart for all parts of the game.

Activity 2

Create your game using your plan.

Activity 3

Keep a record of any errors you found and how you fixed them.

Activity 4

Create a test plan for your game.

Make sure you use normal, extreme and erroneous tests (where appropriate).

Activity 5

Test your game using your test plan.

If you find any problems, debug them, and re-test them to prove it now works.

Activity 6

Choose an additional feature to add to your game.

Create a plan and flowchart for your new feature.

Implement your new feature.

Test your new feature.

Reflection

1 Explain how variables can be used in a program.

_____

_____

_____

_____

_____

_____

2 Identify two real-life examples of where you have encountered 'if' statements in real life, for example the door is locked and it will not open.

_____

_____

_____

_____

_____

_____

3 Explain the importance of random numbers in computers.

_____

_____

_____

_____

_____

_____

	In this module you will:	Pass/Merit	Done?
1	Create a series of connected web pages	P	
2	Include links	P	
3	Insert images	P	
4	Demonstrate user awareness	M	
5	Recognise HTML code.	M	

Did you know?

The first website to go online was the website http://info.cern.ch.

It went online on 6 August 1991.

In this module you are going to learn several exciting website design skills. These skills will help you create a high-quality website about your favourite superheroes for your final project.

You will learn how to write HTML code to create webpages, link webpages together, display images, format text and format backgrounds.

This module shows you how to use the software Notepad to develop your website design skills. Notepad is a simple text-editing program that can also be used to author webpages. It will allow you to type in the code and save the document that you create as a webpage. You will then be able to view your webpage using a web browser.

You will also learn:

- how to create ordered and unordered lists on a webpage.

Before you start

You should be able to:

- understand how to type text into a document
- understand how to create documents for a particular audience and purpose
- use an internet browser.

Introduction

You may use **websites** for many different things. You may use them to read about your favourite things, for social media, to download or stream music and movies, or to play computer games. One of the most important things about any website, whatever it is used for, is that it has a user-friendly design. Have you ever used a website and felt very frustrated that you could not find what you wanted?

If the design for a website is carefully thought out, it can make the experience of using it a positive and pleasing one for the user (or target **audience**). If the design for a website is not carefully considered or the **purpose** is unclear, it can leave the user feeling frustrated and negative about the website.

You are going to learn how to create a **webpage** using **HTML**. You will need to pay close attention to detail as if you make a small error in any of the code you will find that items on your webpage won't display properly.

What is HTML?

HTML is short for Hypertext Markup Language. It is one of the coding languages that can be used to create a webpage. Other coding languages that are sometimes used to create webpages are JavaScript, CSS and PHP, but HTML is one of the oldest and most widely used.

The HTML code that you write is interpreted (read) by a web browser. The web browser makes sure that all the text and images that you want to include in your website are displayed. The web browser makes sure that they are formatted correctly. The web browser will use the code like a guide that tells it where to place the different elements and what they should look like.

Websites need to be written in code so that they can have interactive elements and can be displayed on many different screens and devices. The alternative would be to send the whole webpage as a large image to the user. What kind of issues would there be if this were the case?

Some people use templates to create a webpage. This is to help them create an effective design. You are going to learn how to create a new webpage from the beginning. This will provide you with valuable skills and will allow you to create a webpage exactly how you want it.

Skill 1

Setting up a webpage

The first thing you need to be able to do is set up a webpage using the software Notepad. Notepad can be used for many different things as well as webpages, so you need to write some HTML code to tell it that it is a webpage that you are creating.

The HMTL code that you write is called the webpage **source code**.

Your teacher will show you how to open a new Notepad document.

Key terms

Website: a collection of webpages.

Audience: the people that will look at the webpage.

Purpose: the reason the webpage is created, for example to be entertaining.

Webpage: a single page in a website.

HTML: the language used to create webpages.

Key term

Source code: the HTML code that is written to create a webpage.

You will need to type the following lines of HTML code into the new Notepad document.

```
<!DOCTYPE html>
<html>
<head>
</head>
<body>
</body>
</html>
```

The code that you have typed is the basic structure for the webpage. It is important to be very accurate when typing the code. Any small errors will often mean that the webpage will not be displayed correctly. This includes making sure that there are no spaces between the angular brackets **<>** and the text between them.

<!DOCTYPE html> tells the software that the type of document you are creating is an HTML document. This tells the software that it will be a webpage.

The angular brackets (**<>**) at the start and end of each line of code create a **tag**. You use tags in Notepad to tell the software what you want it to display and how you want it to be displayed.

<html> is an **opening tag**. This is used to tell the software where the webpage starts.

<head> is an opening tag for the header section. The head section is used for things such as the title of the page, and will appear in the tab at the top of the webpage.

</head> is the **closing tag** for the header section. You can see the difference between the opening and closing tags as closing tags start with a forward slash (/).

Key terms

Tag: a piece of code that is used to add content and styling to a webpage.

Opening tag: the tag that goes at the start of the content.

Closing tag: the tag that goes at the end of the content.

`<body>` is an opening tag for the body section. The body section is where all the content for the webpage is written.

`</body>` is the closing tag for the body section.

`</html>` is a closing html tag. This is used to tell the software where the webpage ends.

Most things that you want to display in HTML code will have an opening tag and a closing tag.

Once you have set up the structure for your website you can start to add content to it.

One of the first things that you should add to each webpage is a title. This won't appear on the actual webpage, it will appear on the tab in the web browser when the webpage is opened.

Adding a title

Type the following code between the **head** tags for your webpage:

`<title>`Test Webpage`</title>`

It should now look like this:

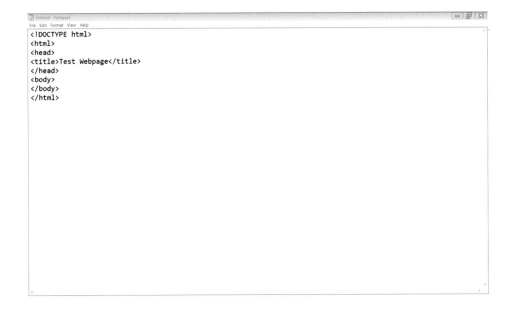

```
<!DOCTYPE html>
<html>
<head>
<title>Test Webpage</title>
</head>
<body>
</body>
</html>
```

Saving the document as a webpage

This is very important:

To be able to see the webpage you have created, you need to save the document in a special way. It needs to be saved as an HTML file.

1 Click on **File** and then 'Save As'.

2 Make sure you save your webpage into an appropriate folder.

3 Type in a suitable filename for the webpage followed by '.html'. For example:
My_Webpage.html

4 When you have typed in the filename, click on Save.

You need to save your file every time you make a change in the code you are writing. You can use the Save option to do this.

You should now be able to open the document as a webpage.

If you go to your documents and find the file that you saved, you should now see the file has a web browser icon next to it.

If you are using Google Chrome it will look like this:

If you click on the file it will open the webpage in a web browser.

You won't see any content on the page yet as you haven't added any. You should see that the title you added is displayed in the tab at the top.

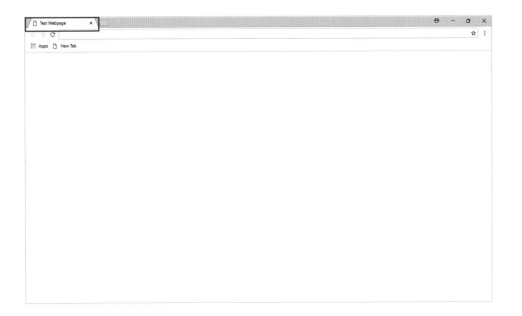

Activity 1.1

Create a folder in a suitable place on your computer and name it 'Website'.

Inside this folder, create another folder and name it 'Images'.

You will save your webpages in the folder called 'Website' and the images for your website in the folder called 'Images'.

Activity 1.2

Set up a webpage with the title 'Homepage'. The homepage is the main webpage of a website.

Use the code in **Skill 1: Adding a title**, as a template to help you.

Remember to save your code in your website folder.

Adding text to a webpage

To create a fun and exciting webpage you need to be able to add text to it. There are two kinds of text: heading text and paragraph text.

These kinds of text form the body of a web page and are inserted between the **<body>** start tag and the **</body>** end tag.

Heading text is what you will use to add any titles or subtitles to your webpages.

Paragraph text is what you will use to add all other text to your webpages.

To add a title to your webpage you will use the heading tag **<h1>**.

To add any subtitles to your webpage you will use the heading tag **<h2>**.

These go within the body tags.

For example:

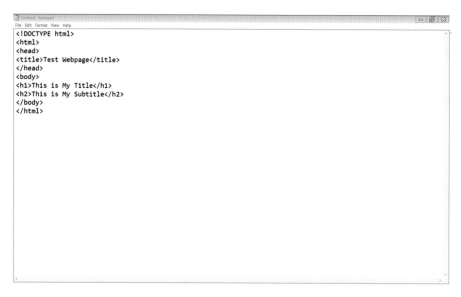

Tip

You will need an opening and closing tag. Any title or subtitle will go in between them.

To add all other text to your webpage you will use the paragraph tag **<p>**.

For example:

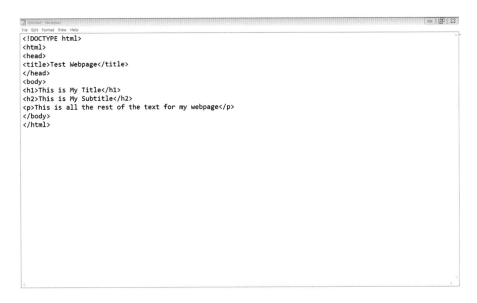

The heading tag and the paragraph tag have a **default setting** for **formatting**. However, you can change the formatting of both. You will learn about this in **Skill 5**.

Activity 2.1

Open your initial webpage and add the heading 'This is my homepage' between **<h1>** and **</h1>** body tags.

Activity 2.2

Look at the screenshot at the start of this page and add some text between **<p>** and **</p>** body tags. End with 'Making webpages is awesome because…'.

Key terms

Navigation: this is what is used to move to the different webpages of a website.

Hyperlinks: links that can be clicked to navigate a website.

Attribute: this is a characteristic of an element that is added to the webpage, for example a certain font.

Anchor: the text that is used for a link. It is the anchor text that is clicked to follow the link.

Getting around!

One thing that can leave a user feeling frustrated is poor **navigation**. It must be easy and simple for the user to find what they are looking for in the website and move between the different webpages in your website. This means that menu options need to be clear and concise. An example of this could be a webpage that contains a company's contact details. Which of the following three menu options do you think would be the best for this and why?

- Details
- Contact information
- Address and other contact details

Now you have learnt how to create a webpage, you will need a way to connect your webpages to create a website. You will do this using **hyperlinks (links)**.

To make a word or multiple words into a link you need to use the following line of code:

```
<a href="webpage.html">link text</a>
```

The opening tag means that you want to add a link.

The **`href` attribute** tells the software where you want to link to. In this case it is to a file called 'webpage.html'.

You need to make sure that all the webpages that you create are saved in the same folder. If they are then you can just use the name of the file for the link.

The 'link text' is the word or words that you want the user to click on as the navigation. This is called the **anchor**.

To create navigation for your website you will need to think of a suitable name for each webpage that you create.

You can then put the names for each webpage at the top of each webpage and add links that will take you to the matching webpage when you click on the link.

For example:

A website could have three pages: a Homepage, an Information page and a Contact us page. At the top of each page it could have the following links:

Homepage   Information   Contact us

Each of these could be made into a link that will take the user to the correct page when the link is clicked.

Add navigation links to another website

You can also link to other websites in this way as well.

For example:

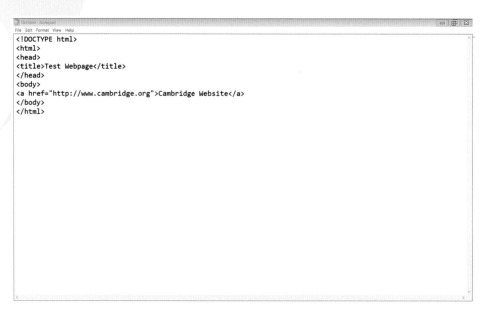

If the user clicked the text 'Cambridge Website', they would be taken to the website in the tag.

Activity 3.1

Your teacher will give you the following webpages: 'Bees_Homepage.html', 'Bees_Info.html' and 'Bees_Contact.html'.

Open the file 'Bees_Homepage.html' and add the following text to the top, just below the body tag:

Homepage   Information   Contact us

Make each page a link to the correct webpage.

'Information' should link to the webpage 'Bees_Info.html' and 'Contact us' should link to 'Bees_Contact.html'.

Make sure that you have all three webpages saved in the same folder.

Activity 3.2

Add the same links to the webpages 'Bees_Info.html' and 'Bees_Contact.html'. You could simply copy and paste the code that you created for 'Bees_Homepage.html' into the correct place for the other two webpages.

Activity 3.3

Open the file 'Bees_Homepage.html' again. Look for the text:

'For more information about bees click here.'

Make the text 'click here' a link to a website about bees. Use the internet to find a suitable website that gives information about bees.

Skill 4

Adding images to a webpage

You have learnt how to set up your webpage and add text to it. You will now learn how to add images.

To add an image to a website you will need to have the image saved in the correct place. You need to save the image in the Images folder that you created earlier. You need to save the image with a suitable filename.

When choosing your image, you need to think about the **quality** of the image. If you choose a low-quality image, it won't look very good on your webpage. However, if you choose a high-quality image, the file size will be a very large and it may take a long time for someone to open your webpage. You will need to decide what is most important to you.

When you have saved the images in the image folder you can insert them into your webpage.

To insert an image

Type the following line of HTML code into the body of the webpage:

```
<img src="****************">
```

If the image was saved in the same folder as the webpages then all you need is the name of the image and its type, here bee.jpg.

This line of code doesn't need a closing tag as the content that gets displayed is put inside the opening tag.

The **'img src'** part is short for 'image source'.

> **Key term**
>
> **Image quality:** this is how good an image looks.

> **WATCH OUT**
>
> Be careful if you are taking images from the internet. Make sure that the sites you want to visit are safe.

This tells the software where to find the image that you want to display. The part that is in the quotation marks is the place where the image is saved and the filename that it is saved as. So, in this example it is saved in the Images folder, that is inside the Website folder, with the filename robot.png.

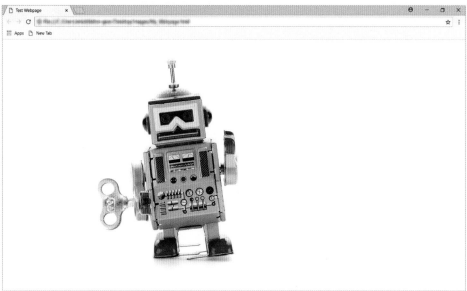

The image will display on the webpage at the size that it is saved. If you want to change the **image size** you need to add some further information to the tag.

The width and the height are the size in **pixels** that you want to display the image.

For example:

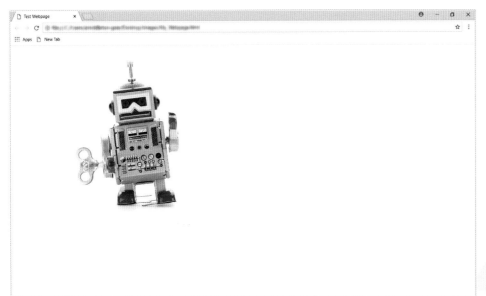

WATCH OUT

You need to be careful when changing the size of an image that you do not distort it.

Key terms

Image size: the height and width measurements of an image.

Pixel: this is a tiny dot or point. Lots of pixels make up an image.

You may also want to change where the image is displayed on the webpage. It will automatically display under the last line of code that you have typed, at the left side of the webpage.

If you want to display it in a different place you can change this using the float attribute.

For example:

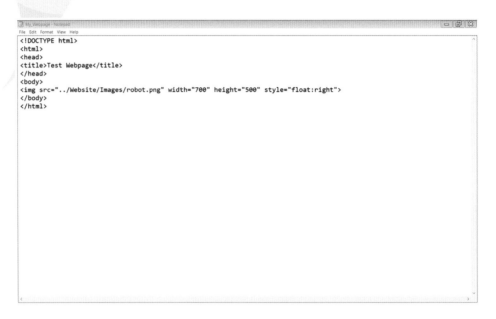

```
<!DOCTYPE html>
<html>
<head>
<title>Test Webpage</title>
</head>
<body>
<img src="../Website/Images/robot.png" width="700" height="500" style="float:right">
</body>
</html>
```

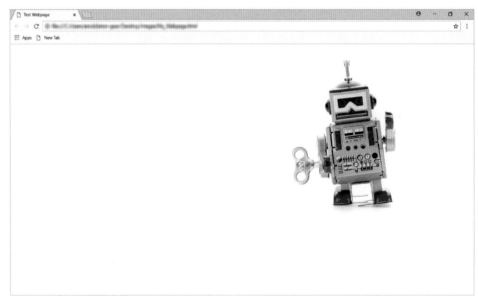

You need to make sure the line of code for the image is placed above the line of code for the text that you want to display it at the side of.

For example:

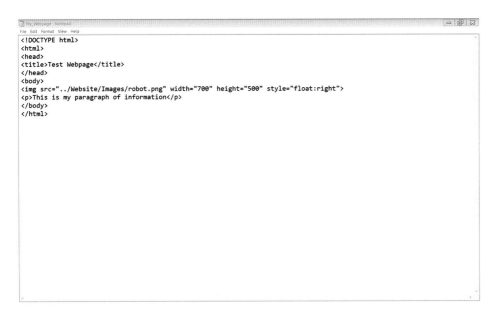

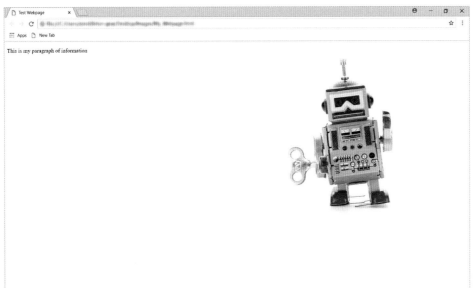

Activity 4.1

Save the image 'Website_Image.jpg' in the Images folder that you created earlier. Save it with the filename 'My_Website_Image.jpg'.

Activity 4.2

Type the HTML code into your webpage to display the image below the text. Remember to include the full location of the image.

Skill 5

What makes a good webpage design

The design layout of a website is very important. It is important that the user can easily read information or use a feature of the website. It is often said that good website design should not make the user think too much! This means that it should be very obvious to the user what is in front of them on the webpage.

Another important factor in the design of a webpage is good use of white space. If there is too much information squeezed onto a webpage, it can make it very difficult for the user to find what they are looking for. It is better to spread the information across several webpages, making it much easier for the user to read.

You will need to think carefully about where each piece of text or image is placed on the webpage. Webpages are often designed so that the information or images that the company wants the user to see first are placed near the top of the page.

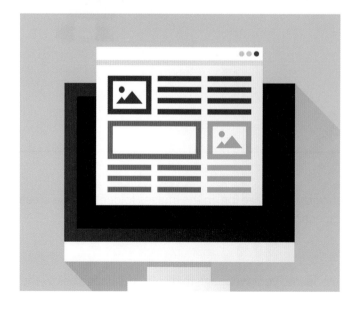

It is important to make sure that a webpage is interesting and appealing for the user to look at. This will maintain the user's attention and improve the experience for them. Information should therefore be presented in different ways, such as text, images, audio, video and graphics (for example graphs and charts).

Another thing to consider to make sure a website design is effective, is that it may be viewed on many different devices, for example PCs, laptops, tablets and mobile phones; therefore, it must be effective for all these devices.

Sometimes websites will change slightly depending on the device. Can you think of any websites that you have looked at that change depending on the device that you are using? What is it that changes? Why do you think these changes are made?

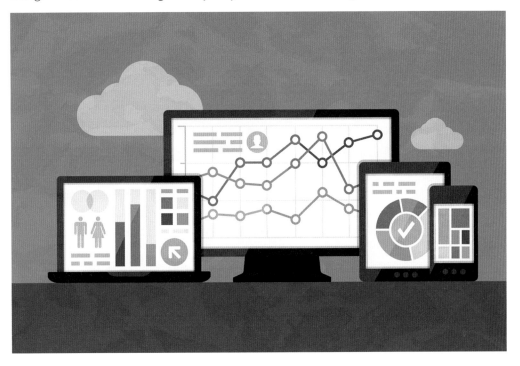

Changing the text formatting

It is important to use the same rules that you have used when creating other documents, such as not using too many different fonts, not using too many different colours and making sure that images are not distorted. This will help your website look more formal.

You should try and keep the style of text simple on a webpage. If text looks too fancy it can be distracting and difficult to read. However, you may want to change the style of the text to suit your audience.

To change the formatting of text you need to add extra information into the opening tag. To do this you use a style attribute. This information will tell the software how you want the text to be displayed on the webpage.

For example:

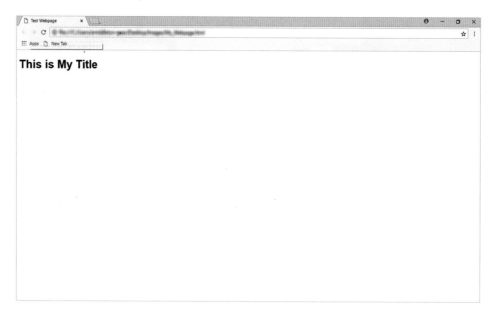

The font-family information tells the software that you want to display the text in a particular font.

Here, the font Arial has been chosen to format the text.

A semicolon is always added to the end to tell the software that it is the end of the formatting for that section.

The formatting that you add to the style attribute needs to be written between quotation marks.

For example:

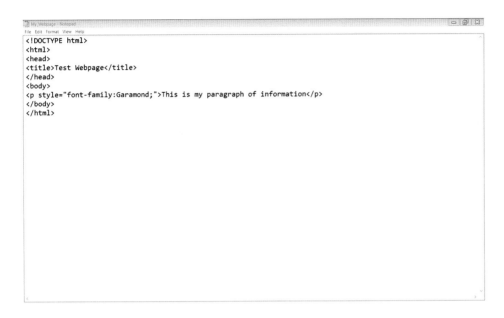

A web browser will only support certain font styles. The most commonly **supported fonts** are:

- Arial
- Bookman Old Style
- Courier New
- Garamond
- Georgia
- Helvetica
- Times New Roman
- Verdana.

Key term

Supported fonts: these are fonts that can be displayed by all web browsers.

Changing the size of the text

You can add further information to the style attribute, such as the font size for the text. This information is added after the semicolon at the end of the font style formatting.

For example:

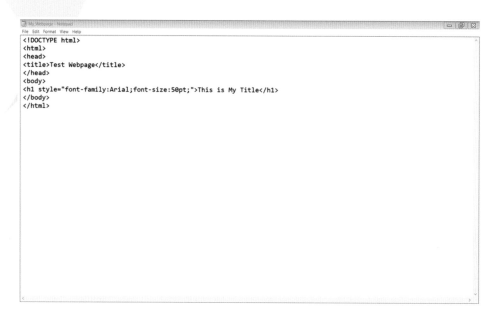

Each formatting choice should be separated by a semicolon and all the formatting choices should be inside the quotation marks.

Changing the colour of the text

You can change the colour of the text using the style attribute.

For example:

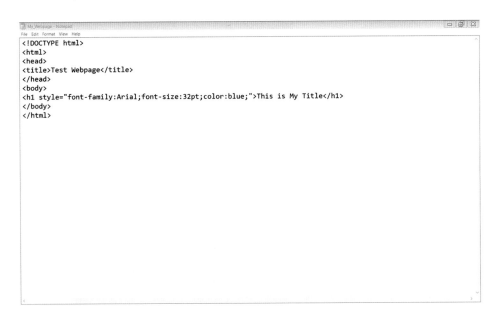

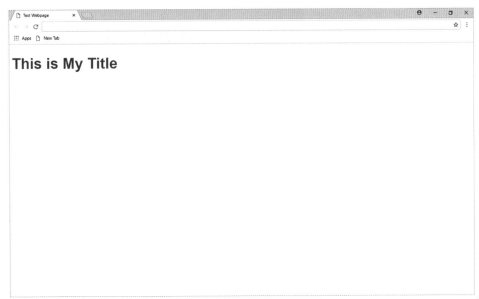

This is My Title

You can type a colour, such as blue, red, green or yellow.

You can even type colours such as lightblue and darkblue, making sure they are all one word.

> **Tip**
>
> You need to note the spelling of 'colour'. It is spelt the American way as 'color' and not 'colour'. If your text is not displaying in the colour that you want, this is a common mistake to check for. Check your spelling!

You can also use something called a hexadecimal colour code. This is a special code that is given to each colour. The code is usually made up of numbers and letters. You can find the hexadecimal colour code for any colour on the internet. Some example codes are:

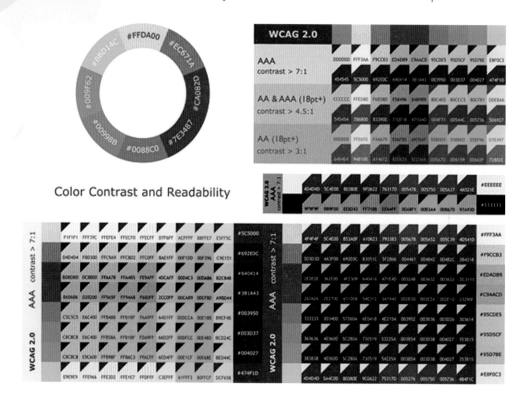

Color Contrast and Readability

For example:

Using a hexadecimal colour code:

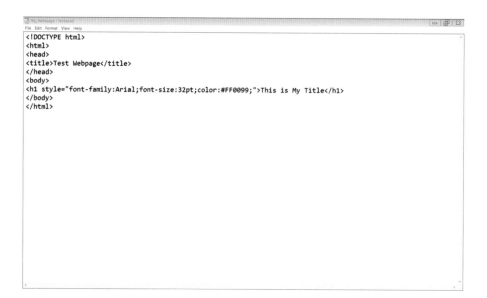

```
<!DOCTYPE html>
<html>
<head>
<title>Test Webpage</title>
</head>
<body>
<h1 style="font-family:Arial;font-size:32pt;color:#FF0099;">This is My Title</h1>
</body>
</html>
```

Tip
You need to remember to put a hashtag (#) before the colour code to tell the software that it is a colour code that you are using.

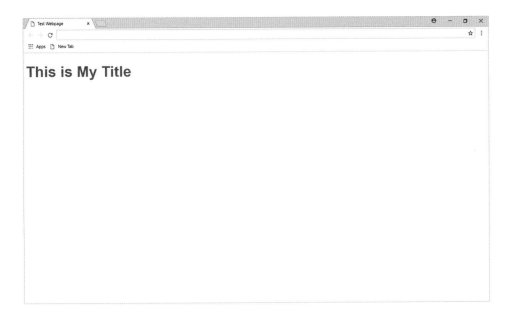

Positioning text

You can also change where the text appears on the page. This is called changing the **alignment** of the text.

To change the alignment of the text you need to add further information to the style attribute.

For example:

All the information in this opening tag will mean that the text will be displayed in font style Arial, at font size 32pt, in the colour pink and in the centre of the page.

Key term

Alignment: this is where the content is placed on the webpage. It could be left, centre or right.

Tip

You should also note the spelling of 'centre'. It is spelt the American way as 'center' and not 'centre'.

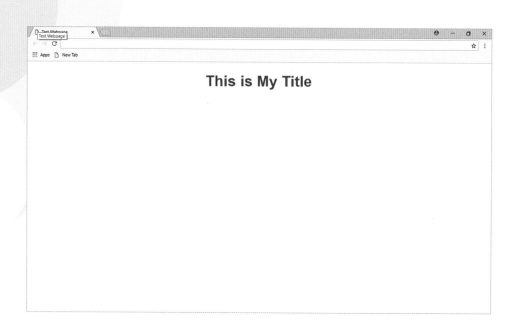

You can also use left and right to display the text at the left or the right. Text will automatically display at the left if no alignment is set.

Formatting the background of a webpage

You are getting very skilled at creating webpages now and hopefully you are finding it fun and challenging.

As well as changing the colour of your text, you can also change the background colour of your webpage to make it look even more interesting.

To change the background colour you need to add some further information to the body tag for the webpage.

For example:

```
<!DOCTYPE html>
<html>
<head>
<title>Test Webpage</title>
</head>
<body style="background-color:lightblue">
</body>
</html>
```

This will make the background colour of the webpage light blue.

You should make sure that the background colour that you use doesn't make the text on your website difficult to read. It is better to use lighter background colours for this reason.

If you do choose a background colour that is a dark colour, you will need to use a light colour for the text to make sure that it can be seen. Although you can read white text on a dark background, it would be tiring to read a lot of text like this. It is often more suitable for headings rather than your main paragraphs of text.

You can also change the background colour behind any heading or paragraph of text. You can use the same code and place it inside the tag for the text.

For example:

```
<!DOCTYPE html>
<html>
<head>
<title>Test Webpage</title>
</head>
<body>
<p style="font-family:Garamond;color:white;background-color:darkblue">This is my paragraph of information</p>
</body>
</html>
```

Activity 5.1

Look at the following two lines of HTML code. Write down how they will display the text.

```
<h1 style="font-family:Garamond;font-size:24pt;
color:#FF0000;text-align:right;">This Is My Title</h1>
```

_____

_____

```
<p style="font-family:Verdana;font-size:18pt;color:lightgreen;
text-align:center;">This is my paragraph</h1>
```

_____

_____

Activity 5.2

Look at the following two lines of HTML, they contain errors. Find the errors.

```
<h1 style=font-family:Arial;font-size:24pt,colour:red;text-
align:center;>This Is My Heading<h1>
```

_____

_____

```
<p style="font-family:Garamond;font-size 18pt;
color:darkblue;text-align:left>This is my paragraph</p>
```

_____

_____

Activity 5.3

Open the webpage you have been working on and format the title so that it is font style Arial.

Activity 5.4

Format the title so that it is also size 24pt, dark blue and will appear in the centre at the top of the webpage.

Activity 5.5

Format the paragraph you wrote in **Skill 2** so that it is size 18pt, font style Garamond, colour 0000FF. Make it appear at the left side of the webpage.

Activity 5.6

Change the background colour of the webpage that you have created to colour FFCCFF.

Activity 5.7

Change the background colour for the paragraph of text on your webpage to white.

Activity 5.8

Save your code and check how it looks when you open it in a web browser. This will show you the effects of all of your changes.

Scenario

Superheroes are awesome!

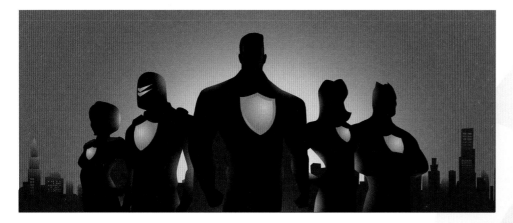

The local comic book store wants a website that tells people about different comic book superheroes. They have given you a file called 'Heroes_Homepage.html'. This is the website that they have created so far. They want you to format this webpage with some information that they have given you.

Activity 1

Open the file 'Heroes_Homepage.html' that your teacher will give you. Make the title of the webpage dark blue, size 36pt and Arial.

Activity 2

Make the other text on the webpage black, size 18pt and Garamond.

Activity 3

Insert the image 'Heroes.jpg' that your teacher will give you. Change the size of the image to be 500 pixels wide by 300 pixels high. Display the image at the right side of the webpage and the text at the left side.

Activity 4

Make the background colour of the website light blue.

Activity 5

Find the text 'List of Superheroes'. Make this text a link to a website that has a list of superheroes.

Tip

You could use the list of superheroes on the Encyclopaedia Britannica website.

Challenge 1
Adding lists

You are going to learn a further skill for your website: adding lists.

Key terms

Ordered list: a list that has numbered bullet points.

Unordered list: a list that has bullet points but no numbers.

You should already be able to create lists on the computer using bullet points. You can create two kinds of lists on a website, these are called **ordered lists** and **unordered lists**. An ordered list will have numbered bullet points, for example:

1 List item 1
2 List item 2
3 List item 3

An unordered list will just have simple bullet points, for example:

- List item
- List item
- List item

To create an ordered list, you will need to use the following code:

```
<ol>
    <li>List item 1</li>
    <li>List item 2</li>
    <li>List item 3</li>
</ol>
```

The **ol** tag means that you want to add an ordered list. This tells the software to put a number at the start of each item in the list. The **li** tag means that you want to add an item to the list. You can see this list has three items. You need to remember to open and close the tags for each item and for the list itself.

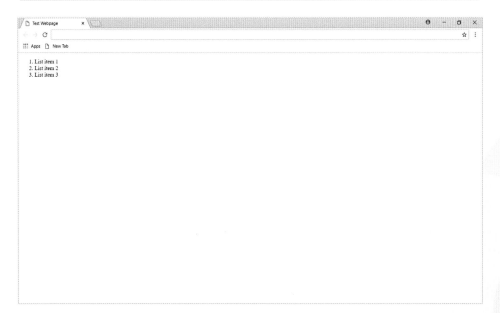

You create an unordered list in a similar way, but rather than using the **ol** tag you need to use the **ul** tag instead. This means that it is an unordered list.

For example:

```
My_Webpage - Notepad
File  Edit  Format  View  Help
<!DOCTYPE html>
<html>
<head>
<title>Test Webpage</title>
</head>
<body>
<ul>
<li>List item 1</li>
<li>List item 2</li>
<li>List item 3</li>
</ul>
</body>
</html>
```

This tells the software to put a bullet point at the start of each item in the list rather than a number.

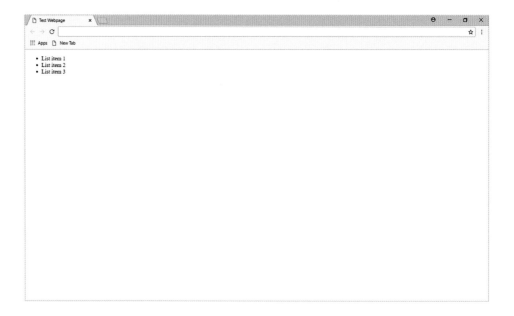

Activity 1

Open your superheroes homepage. Add an unordered list of the ten most popular superheroes.

Activity 2

Add an ordered list, ranking your top five superheroes.

Challenge 2

Publishing to the World Wide Web

For everyone else to be able to see a website that has been created, it needs to be published to the World Wide Web. When it is published it will be given a **domain name**. This is the name that is given to the webpage that people can type into the address bar of their web browser, to find the webpage.

To publish a website, you need to find someone to host it. When a website is hosted it is placed on a webserver and given a special address, called an **IP address**, so that other people can access the website. A special computer, called a **Domain Name Server**, will match the domain name for the website that the user types in, to the IP address, so that the correct webpage information is sent to the user.

In this module, you will not be going as far as publishing the webpages that you create. If you were to publish your website, however, there are several things that you would need to think about.

> **Key terms**
>
> **Domain name:** the name used to identify an IP address.
>
> **IP address:** a unique address given to a device when it connects to the internet.
>
> **Domain Name Server:** a directory or database of all the domain names and their matching IP addresses.

Activity 1

Ask yourself the following questions:

- Do you need to get any permission to publish the text that you have included?
- Do you need to get any permission to publish any images that you have included?
- Is the information that you have included non-offensive to different people and cultures?
- Have you included any information about yourself that could put you at risk?
- Have you included any information about anyone else that could put them at risk?

By making sure that you have thought about these things, you have shown **ethical behaviour** when publishing a website.

> **Key term**
>
> **Ethical behaviour:** behaving in a way that shows moral principles. It is seen as good and honest behaviour.

Final project – Who's your favourite superhero?

The comic book store wants you to add a further three webpages about your favourite superheroes to the website. You can make the webpages as fun and exciting as you like!

Activity 1

Create three more webpages to add to the superhero website.

You could use the same style that the comic book store gave you or you could create your own style. If you choose to create your own style, make sure that you change the style for the homepage to match it.

Activity 2

Add navigation links to each webpage to make sure that the user can navigate to and from each webpage.

Activity 3

List three features of your website that make it more suitable for your audience.

Activity 4

List three features of your website that make it more suitable for the purpose.

Reflection

1 Why is it important to keep the design of a website simple?

_____

_____

_____

2 What can you do to make sure that your website looks formal?

_____

_____

_____

3 Why is it important to pay very close attention to the HTML code?

_____

_____

_____

	In this module you will:	Pass/Merit	Done?
1	Design a simple network	P	
2	Identify the purpose and components of a network	P	
3	Demonstrate understanding of management issues associated with networks	M	
4	Understand network security issues.	M	

In this module you are going to develop skills to help you work towards your final project which is to plan a computer network for a school. To be able to complete this project, you will need to learn what a **network** of devices is and the devices that are combined to create a network.

Key terms

Network: two or more computers connected together to communicate.

Topology: the layout of a network.

Planning the structure of a network for a specific situation will be vital, as will identifying the devices that are needed to create the network. You will also learn about network **topologies** (the layout of a network), where the devices are and what they are connected to. It will be important to recognise the management issues associated with the network you have designed and the possible security issues.

You will also learn:

• about the uses of networks

• about network topologies.

Before you start

You should:

- be aware of what is meant by a hardware device, and be able to identify a range of hardware devices such as keyboard, mouse, laptop, mobile phone
- be aware that computers can be joined together to communicate and know some of the reasons why this is done.

Introduction

When one or more devices are connected, they create a network. This could be as small as a mobile phone connecting to another mobile phone using **Bluetooth**, to 100 computers connected in a school, all the way up to the **internet** and the millions of devices that connect together across the world.

Skill 1

Purpose of a network

Computers can be joined together for lots of different reasons, but it is always about communication. Computers have the ability to send data to each other, whether this data is text, images or videos – it is all data, and it can all be sent on a network.

Networks might have single or multiple purposes.

Single purpose

This could be a laptop connecting to a printer, for example. The laptop will send data to the printer (the document(s) to print). The printer will send data to the laptop to give it information, for example telling the computer it is ready to print, or if it is out of paper.

Multiple purpose

A network of computers in a business can have lots of purposes. There might be a central store of data that the employees (the people who work at the business) want to access from their own computers. It will allow the employees to communicate with each other, for example by sending emails. It might allow employees to access the internet so they can access websites and contact customers.

Key terms

Bluetooth: a method of wireless data transmission.

Internet: The internet is a global collection of networks connecting computers and other hardware together to provide the infrastructure needed to access the World Wide Web.

Personal Area Network (PAN): a small network set up for a specific purpose.

Local Area Network (LAN): a network over a small geographical area, using business-owned or personally owned hardware.

Wide Area Network (WAN): a network that connects computers and LANs over a large geographic area using cables, fibre optics, or satellites, and can span cities, countries, or the globe.

Password: a series of characters that are needed to gain access to a system.

Types of network

Networks can be put into different categories.

Personal Area Network (PAN)

A **Personal Area Network (PAN)** is a small network, usually between a small number of devices. It is set up for a specific purpose such as a Bluetooth connection between two mobile phones or a connection between a laptop and a printer (or scanner).

Local Area Network (LAN)

A **Local Area Network (LAN)** is a set of computers that are connected over a small geographical area. The hardware used in the network is provided and maintained by the person or company, for example they use their own cables to join the computers. This could include devices connected in a home or the devices connected in a single building.

Wide Area Network (WAN)

A **Wide Area Network (WAN)** is a set of computers that are connected over a large geographical area – it could be across an entire country or across the world. The hardware is not owned by the person or company using it, but they use the telephone lines and fibre optic cables that form the internet to send the data. This could be a nationwide bank, for example, that has dozens of branches across the country. A WAN is owned and run by a specific company, and you usually need a username and **password** to access it.

The internet

This is the hardware that connects computers worldwide. It is the cables, satellites, routers, switches and other devices that join computers within a country and between countries. The **internet** is actually just a WAN made up of lots of smaller WANs and LANs that all join together.

Some people confuse this with the **World Wide Web (WWW)**. The WWW is the websites that you can visit by using the internet.

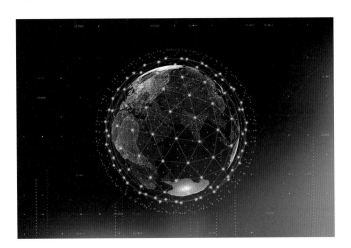

Activity 1.1

Make a list of all the occasions when you have sent data from one device to another. This might be to open a website, to send an email to a teacher or friend, or to print a document.

_____

_____

_____

_____

_____

Compare your list to a friend's and add any you had missed to your own list.

Activity 1.2

For each of the activities you identified in **Activity 1.1**, identify whether you were using a PAN, LAN, WAN or the internet. You might have used a combination of these, for example accessing a website may have used a LAN and then the internet.

Activity 1.3

Your school might have one, or more, networks.

Does your school have a PAN, LAN or WAN? Or does it have more than one?

_____

Can you access the internet from your school's computers?

_____

Write down all the occasions when you (and other people) use your school's network.

_____

_____

_____

_____

Skill 2

Components of a network

A network can be made up of different pieces of hardware. These are called the **components** of the network. Each device has its own purpose within a network, and they are not all used in every network. All computers that are connected in the network, and all devices that are used to connect the computers in a network (e.g. switch, hub), are known as **nodes**.

Cables

A **cable** physically connects two devices together. There are two types of cable: copper and fibre optic.

Copper cable transfers data using electrical signals. There are lots of different types of cable:

- **Unshielded Twisted Pair (UTP)**. This is two copper cables twisted together without any shielding.
- Shielded Twisted Pair (STP). This is two copper cables twisted together with shielding to reduce **interference**.

In a network, the cable most commonly used is called an **ethernet** cable. You can get these in different lengths, and in different colours.

The ethernet cable plugs into a **jack**.

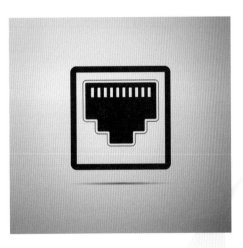

Key terms

Copper cable: a cable connection that can be UTP or STP. Data is transferred as electricity.

Unshielded Twisted Pair (UTP): two pieces of copper cables that are twisted together. There is no shielding against interference.

Interference: an interruption or disruption to a signal when it's being sent. This could change the binary value being transmitted, creating an incorrect signal.

Ethernet: a specific type of copper cable used in a network.

Jack: the component an ethernet cable plugs into.

Fibre optic cable transfers data using light. This can send data faster than a copper cable as it has a higher **bandwidth**. Fibre optic is more expensive than copper cable.

Hub

When there are lots of computers connected, they can each connect to a **hub**. If Computer A wants to send a message to Computer B, it sends it to the hub. The hub then sends the message to all the computers connected to it. All computers get the message but only Computer B reads what it says.

Switch

A **switch** has the same purpose as a hub. It connects devices together but works slightly differently. The switch records the identity of each computer that sends it a message. Once Computer A sends a message to the switch, the switch knows where Computer A is. If Computer B sends a message for Computer A to the switch, it goes straight to that computer, and that computer only.

Router

A **router** is also a device that connects computers, but it can also connect different networks together.

If a computer on Network A needs to send a message to a computer on Network B, then the two networks need to be connected. This could be through the internet, or by directly connecting the networks using a device such as a router. The router receives the message from Network A and forwards it onto Network B.

Key terms

Router: a component that connects computers and networks together.

Modem: a component that allows connection to the internet using a telephone line.

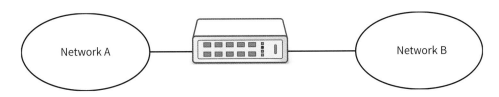

A router might also have a modem inside it.

Modem

Modem stands for modulator-demodulator. It allows you to connect to the internet using a telephone cable. It converts the analogue sound waves from the telephone line into digital data that a computer can understand, and vice-versa.

Network Interface Card (NIC)

Ethernet cables need to connect to a device. They plug into a **Network Interface Card (NIC)** on your computer. Without a NIC you cannot connect physically to a network. These are often built into devices.

Wireless Access Point (WAP)

More and more devices are connecting **wirelessly** which means using radio waves to send the data. A **Wireless Access Point (WAP)** can send and receive messages wirelessly. This can be added onto other devices, for example a switch. The switch can now receive messages wirelessly, and send wireless messages to devices.

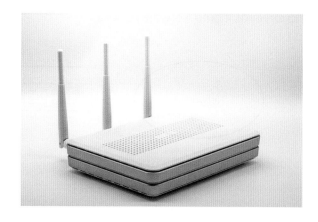

Wireless Network Interface Card (WNIC)

A computer also needs to send and receive data wirelessly. A **Wireless Network Interface Card (WNIC)** performs the same tasks as a NIC but it sends and receives the data using radio waves instead of along physical cables. These are usually built into devices.

Server

A **server** is a central computer that can perform lots of tasks for the network, for example managing the traffic, controlling access through usernames, passwords and access rights.

A server has different functions:

- **File server:** this can store data. That means all computers on the network can access the data on the server.

- **Print server:** a printer is attached to the server. Any computer on the network can print to this printer. The data goes to the server, then the server decides which order to print the documents.
- **Email server:** in a business you might have your business email address. The email server manages these email accounts and stores all your emails. If you want to read your emails, then you need to connect to the email server.

Activity 2.1

Find out if your school's network has any of the devices shown in **Skill 2**. Write down the names of the devices.

Activity 2.2

Find out if your school's network has any network devices <u>not</u> described here. Write down the names of these devices and then find out what they do.

Activity 2.3

There are five different network components described below. Write down which component you think is being described.

1 A component that allows you to connect to the internet using a telephone line.

_____

2 A component that connects computers together. When it receives a message it always sends it to every computer connected to it.

_____

3 A component that is attached to your computer. It allows you to send and receive data wirelessly.

_____

4 A component that physically joins computers together. It sends data using light.

_____

5 A component that connects computers together, and can join different networks together.

_____

Key terms

Print server: a computer that manages a printer.

Email server: a computer that stores emails for users to access.

Skill 3

Designing a network

Once you know what all the different network components do, you need to choose which you are going to use to create a new network.

You need to ask yourself a set of questions to decide which components are needed.

1: Do you need a server?

You don't always need a server.

- A large organisation might need a server to store its files, emails and so on, and to prevent the need for one printer for every computer.
- A small network, for example in your home, probably won't need a server. Each computer will store its own data, and you can access email online.
- A server is expensive and needs someone with technical skills to maintain it.

2: Wired, wireless or mixed?

Physically connecting devices with cables gives higher bandwidth than wireless. Do you need this extra speed? That depends on the number of computers.

- If you have hundreds of computers all sending and receiving data, then a high bandwidth will be necessary. Also, if you want to transfer large files, for example videos, then a faster bandwidth is better.
- If you have only three or four computers, and you're sending small files then wireless will be sufficient.
- Wireless is also useful if you have portable computers, for example if you have a laptop that you want to use in different rooms, or a tablet computer that you want to connect.
- Wireless is less secure, so important data is more likely to be intercepted.
- Wireless is not always as reliable, walls can get in the way and make the signal weaker.

You can, of course, have a mixture. Some of the computers are connected with cables (wired), and some of the computers are connected wirelessly.

3: Do you need access to the internet and/or another network?

If you are connecting to the internet (using telephone lines) then a modem will be required, or a router with a modem inside it.

If you want to join your network to another network, for example a LAN in another building, then a router will be needed.

> **Tip**
>
> Remember, all computers need to attach to the central device.

4: What will the computers connect to?

Hubs, switches and routers all connect computers together. Which one(s) you choose depends on what you need.

A hub is the cheapest, but it is the least efficient. This is best when there are only a small number of computers to connect.

A switch is more efficient than a hub, but slightly more expensive. This is best where there are more computers, for example 20 computers need to connect to the one device.

A router is the most efficient, but it needs setting up and requires someone to do that. This is best when there are a large number of computers and you need to connect to another network.

Network diagrams

A network diagram shows all the components that you need in the network. It shows the cables that connect computers and the components that these connect to.

There are two different networks described below. There are some examples of questions that you need to ask yourself to make appropriate decisions about the devices and connections needed in the network.

Network 1: a small home network

A family has one desktop computer, two laptops, one tablet and two mobile phones.

Step 1: You will need to consider the following:

1 Do you need a server? *No. This is a small network; each computer will store its own data.*

2 Wired, wireless or mixed? *The laptops, tablet and mobile phones are all portable so they need to be wireless. The desktop computer could be attached wired or wirelessly.*

3 Do you need access to the internet and/or another network? *They need to connect to the internet, so a modem is needed.*

4 What will the computers connect to? *There are only a small number of computers so a hub will be ok.*

Step 2: You will need to draw the devices the family will have and the components you have identified.

Step 3: You can draw lines to connect the devices: solid lines can represent cables and dashed lines can represent wireless.

Step 4: You will then need to label each device.

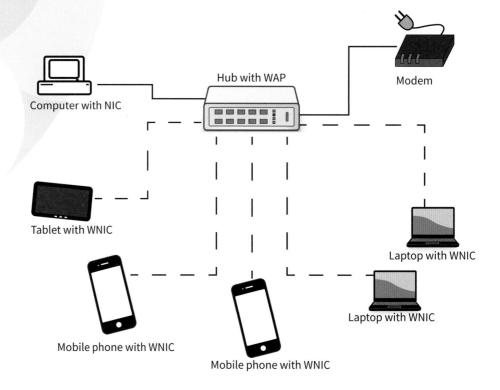

Network 2: a shop

A shop needs to store its data on a central computer. In the front of the shop there are five checkouts: each is an individual computer. In the back of the shop there are offices, with three desktop computers. The manager also has a mobile phone and there are two tablets that are used in the back of the shop. The desktop computers need access to the internet. The server has a printer attached to it for all computers to use.

1. Do you need a server? *Yes. Data needs to be stored centrally.*

2. Wired, wireless or mixed? *The checkouts might have secure data (for example credit card numbers), and need a reliable connection, so wired is better. The desktop computers could be wired or wireless. The tablets and mobile phone need to be wireless.*

3. Do you need access to the internet and/or another network? *They need to connect to the internet, so a modem is needed.*

4. What will the computers connect to? *There are only a small number of computers, but there is a central server so they already need someone to manage the network. They could use a switch or a router to make it more efficient.*

This network has two separate areas, so they could each have their own device to connect to, then these will join together.

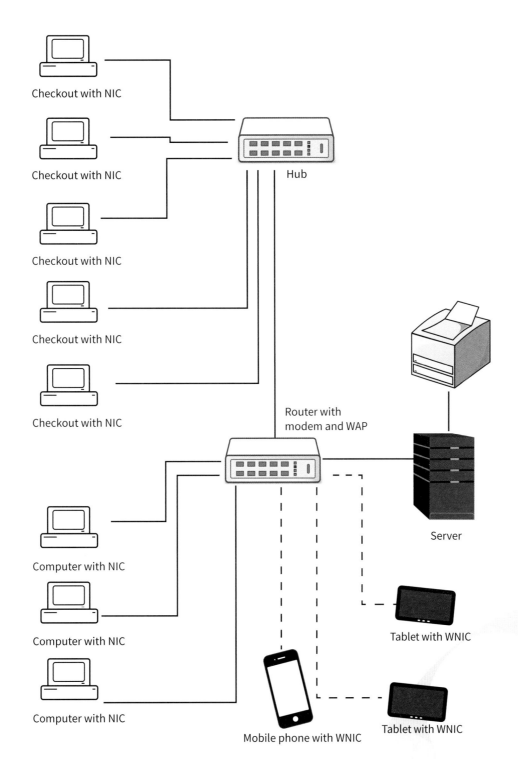

Checkout with NIC

Checkout with NIC

Checkout with NIC

Checkout with NIC

Checkout with NIC

Hub

Router with
modem and WAP

Computer with NIC

Computer with NIC

Computer with NIC

Mobile phone with WNIC

Server

Tablet with WNIC

Tablet with WNIC

Activity 3.1

Three university students live in a shared house. They all need access to the internet. One of the students needs a high bandwidth for their desktop computer. The other two students have laptops. Each student has a mobile phone.

Answer the following questions for this network:

1 Do they need a server?

_____

2 Wired, wireless or mixed?

_____

3 Do they need access to the internet and/or another network?

_____

4 What will the computers connect to?

_____

Draw a network plan for the house.

Make sure you label all the devices.

Tip

You can use software to draw network diagrams if you don't want to do them by hand or on a word processor. You could use: Dia Diagram Editor, Calligra Flow, Microsoft Visio or Cisco Packet Tracer.

Activity 3.2

A business has ten employees. The three managers each have desktop computers in the office, they also each have a tablet computer. The remaining seven employees each have a laptop. The business has its own email system that is managed on the network, and all employees need to access the same files that are stored centrally. The business needs to access the internet.

Answer the following questions for this network:

1 Do they need a server?

_____

2 Wired, wireless or mixed?

_____

3 Do they need access to the internet and/or another network?

_____

4 What will the computers connect to?

_____

Draw a network plan for the business.

Make sure you label all the devices.

Skill 4

Identifying management tasks

Networks, especially large networks, need managing. This is usually performed by network experts who look after the network, fix any problems and make sure it runs efficiently and securely.

The table gives some network management tasks:

Management task	Description
Hardware management	Looking after the hardware that makes up the network. This could include: • setting up new devices • repairing devices • replacing devices.
Software management	Looking after the software that runs on the network. Some networks need specific Network Operating Systems to allow them to run. Software management could include: • installing software on the computers that connect to the network • installing software on the server • **updating** software • **upgrading** software.
User management	Networks can have user accounts that people have to log into. The user management could include: • creating new accounts • managing each user's area on the server • giving specific **access rights** to individual users.

Key terms

Updating: installing a new feature, or fix for a fault, to a piece of software you already have.

Upgrading: installing a completely new version of a piece of software.

Access rights: limiting, or allowing, users to perform certain actions. For example a user may not have access to the network.

Management task	Description
Security management	Networks need to be kept secure (see **Skill 5** for more about security). Security management could include: • setting up **firewalls** and **anti-malware** software • running regular anti-malware, e.g. **virus-checker** • setting up **encryption** routines • **backing up** the data regularly.

Key terms

Firewall: hardware or software that prevents unauthorised transmissions.

Anti-malware: software that detects malware and deletes it.

Malware: a piece of software that is on your computer without your knowledge. It might delete your data, or record what you are doing to send it onto someone else.

Virus-checker: an example of anti-malware that looks for, and removes, viruses.

Encryption: data is jumbled using a key so it cannot be understood.

Backup: making a copy of data and storing it elsewhere, in case the original is lost.

Hacker: a person who tries to gain unauthorised access to a system.

Activity 4.1

Write a job advert for a university network manager. Include a description of some of the tasks they will need to perform.

Skill 5

Understand network security issues

Data is valuable and needs to be protected.

A computer network that is unprotected can let unauthorised people gain access, for example **hackers**. They can then read all the data that is stored on the computers in the network. This could include:

• personal information
• private images or copyrighted material
• financial details
• confidential plans.

This data could be used inappropriately to:

- steal someone's identity (identify theft) using their personal information
- steal money using the financial records
- claim that private images or copyrighted material belong to someone else
- use confidential plans to steal and/or sell ideas.

To try and stop this from happening, a network needs security.

Security measure	Description
Firewall	This can be hardware and/or software. It watches the signals coming into, and out of, the network. It blocks any signals that are unauthorised.
Anti-malware	This is software. When it is installed, kept up to date and run regularly, it will check files for malware and then either delete them or put them into quarantine so they can't do any damage.
Encryption	Data is encrypted using a key. This jumbles up the data. If the data is accessed without the key, it is meaningless.
Backup	A backup is a copy of the data that is stored elsewhere. If someone gains access to the network, they might delete (or change) the data. If this happens, the backup can be used to get the correct data back.
Passwords	Passwords should be complex. This usually means they: • are more than eight characters long • include numbers • include capital and lowercase letters • include other symbols, for example #,! or %. The more complex the password, the more possible combinations there could be. This makes it harder for someone to guess it.

Even with security measures in place, they are never guaranteed to work.

Activity 5.1

The business in **Activity 3.2** does not currently have any network security measures in place. Write a letter to the manager of the business telling them why they need to have security measures.

Activity 5.2

The manager has agreed with your points about needing security, but does not know what they should include.

Write a report to the manager, telling them about the security measures they should include, and why the measures will help.

Scenario

Home network

Dinesh has just moved into a new house with his family. He works from home and needs access to the internet. He has two desktop computers in his home office.

Dinesh's family own two laptops, two tablets, and there are four mobile phones. These all need to connect to the network but need to be able to be moved around the home.

Activity 1

Answer the following questions for this network:

1 Do they need a server?

_____

2 Wired, wireless or mixed?

_____

3 Do they need access to the internet and/or another network?

_____

4 What will the computers connect to?

_____

Activity 2

Draw a network plan for Dinesh's home using your answers to **Activity 1**.

Activity 3

Label the components on your network plan.

Activity 4

Create a table that explains to Dinesh what each component in the network plan does.

Activity 5

Write a letter to Dinesh, describing two management tasks that he will need to perform on the network.

Activity 6

Edit your letter from **Activity 5**.

Add a paragraph to tell Dinesh why it is important he considers the security of his network.

Tell Dinesh what he needs to do to help keep his network secure.

Challenge

All the networks shown so far have been **star** networks. This is the network topology. The connecting device (hub, switch or router) is central with all devices connected to it.

There are other topologies that can include switches, but don't always. Here are two other topologies:

1 A **mesh** network topology tries to connect devices to as many other devices as it can.

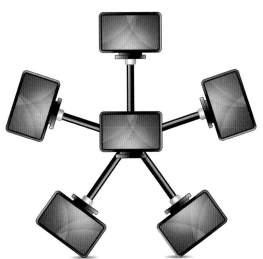

This is good because there are direct connections to more computers, so data can get there faster and directly. However, imagine if there were 100 computers and every computer was connected to every other computer! That would be a lot of cables and it would be very difficult to maintain.

<aside>

Key terms

Star topology: a network where all computers connect to a central component.

Mesh topology: a network where all computers connect to each other.

</aside>

2   A **bus** network topology has a central cable known as the backbone. All devices connect into this single cable. When a signal is sent, it goes onto the backbone and travels to every computer connected to it, but only the computer it is meant for reads it. This is good because there are fewer cables needed, but there are lots of collisions as every computer is sending data down the same cable! When two computers try and do it at the same time, it crashes.

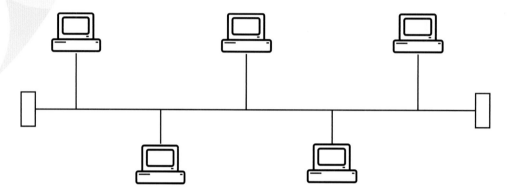

Activity 1

An office has three desktop computers. They want a mesh topology network setting up.

Draw a network plan for the office using a mesh topology.

Activity 2

An office has ten desktop computers. They want a bus topology network setting up.

Draw a network plan for the office using a bus topology.

Final project – School IT department network

Your school has only ever had standalone computers (not networked). It has decided that it needs to allow students access to the internet and would like to install a network to allow students to communicate and to store data on a server instead of the individual computers. The school would like you to plan and design this network for them.

There is one IT classroom. There are 20 desktop computers in it. There is one printer, which is in the classroom, and the school wants this printer to be used by any of the computers.

They have created an IT technician's office that will have two desktop computers. They are going to hire one technician who will have a tablet and mobile phone.

There are four laptop computers in the staff room for teachers, and these need to be able to connect to the network as well.

The school would like all data to be stored centrally in the technician's office.

Activity 1

Answer the following questions for this network:

1 Do they need a server?

_____

2 Wired, wireless or mixed?

_____

3 Do they need access to the internet and/or another network?

_____

4 What will the computers connect to?

_____

Activity 2

Draw a network plan for the school using your answers to **Activity 1**.

Activity 3

Label the components on your network plan.

Write the name of the topology of your network.

Activity 4

Create a table that explains to the Principal what each component in the network plan does.

Activity 5

Write a report to the Principal describing <u>three</u> management tasks that the schools will need to perform on the network.

Activity 6

Edit your letter from **Activity 5**.

Add a paragraph to tell the Principal why it is important the school considers the security of the network.

Tell the Principal what the school needs to do to help keep the network secure.

> **Tip**
>
> There are two rooms in this network. Draw each one as an individual network, then join them together.

Reflection

1 Explain why networks are sometimes more useful than standalone computers.

_____

_____

_____

_____

2 Explain why it is sometimes better to have a standalone computer instead of a network.

_____

_____

_____

_____

3 Explain why it is important to plan a network before trying to set it up.

_____

_____

_____

_____

4 Explain why it is important that a network (and data on a computer) is kept secure.

_____

_____

_____

_____

Video or animation for a purpose

	In this module you will:	Pass/Merit	Done?
1	Create a plan for video or animation	P	
2	Create source material for video or animation	P	
3	Produce video or animation with appropriate software	P	
4	Add soundtrack or narration to video or animation	M	
5	Demonstrate awareness of how the finished media text addresses a specific audience.	M	

In this module you are going to develop skills to help you work towards your final project. This project will be to design and create a video or animation to advertise your school to new students.

You will learn how to create two types of product, and can then choose which you want to use in your final project.

You will also learn how to create and manipulate a sound file (using the software Audacity) to import into your animation or video.

Before you start

You should:

- be able to create images using computer software such as a simple paint package
- know what multimedia is and be able to create multimedia documents.

Introduction

Videos and animations are both examples of moving images.

An **animation** is a series of images that have been hand-drawn or created using a computer. When the images are viewed in a sequence, they look like they are moving. The first animations were created using individual hand-drawn images that were moved quickly to appear as though they were moving. More recently, computer-generated imagery (CGI) is used to create animations entirely using a computer.

Key terms

Animation: a series of hand-drawn or computer-generated images that, when viewed as a sequence, give the impression of movement.

Video: a recording of moving images.

A **video** is a recording of moving images, usually created using a video camera, which produces a digital recording.

You will learn how to create a simple animation using Pencil2D. You will also learn how to create your own video by combining a series of videos and images.

Tip

Don't make your plan too complicated. Keep it simple so you know you can create the animation.

Skill 1

Creating a storyboard

Before you create a video or animation, it is important that you make a plan. This plan is usually called a **storyboard** and is shown on paper. It is a visual representation of your intended video or animation and will show the different parts. You may want to change your plan lots of times, and your final product may not be the same as when you started, but that's ok. A plan is just your first ideas. You can make as many changes as you like, but it gets you thinking, and gets you started.

A storyboard is usually made up for several frames. A **frame** is one still image in a video or animation. You can't draw every still image you want to include, but you can show the main ones. You can then **annotate** the storyboard to show what is going to happen.

Each frame in a storyboard is drawn in one box. Annotations can be used to describe the animation. Each frame should have a number in it so you know the order in which they are viewed.

Key terms

Storyboard: a planning tool using a series of drawings to show what will happen.

Frame: one whole image in an animation or video.

Annotate: writing on a drawing to explain what it shows, or what will happen.

Here is the first frame for an animation you might produce about your hobbies:

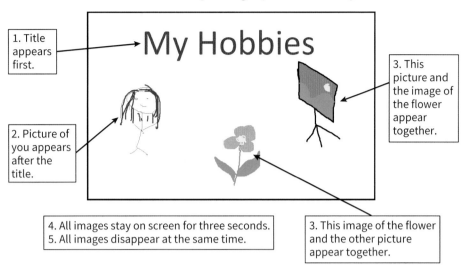

1. Title appears first.

2. Picture of you appears after the title.

3. This picture and the image of the flower appear together.

4. All images stay on screen for three seconds.
5. All images disappear at the same time.

3. This image of the flower and the other picture appear together.

The annotations show that the title appears first and slides in from the left. Then an image of you appears and at the same time an image of a drawing and a flower appear. Items 4 and 5 describe what happens after the images have appeared.

This shows the second frame of your animation:

1. Title slides in from the left.

3. Both flowers grow, starting as green dots and getting larger.

2. The tree grows, starting with the bottom green line and slowly getting larger.

4. All images stay on screen for three seconds.
5. All images disappear at the same time.

> **Tip**
>
> It's not an art competition! If you don't want to draw an image (for example a flower), you could just draw a circle and write 'flower' inside it.
>
> Remember, this is just a plan.

Activity 1.1

You are going to create a short animation about your hobbies. This will be for the rest of the students in your class to tell them about what you enjoy doing.

Plan the first frame of your animation by drawing (and annotating) a storyboard frame.

Activity 1.2

Draw the second frame of your animation. Make sure you annotate the first frame to say how long it stays on screen, how it moves to the second frame, and so on.

Activity 1.3

Continue with your storyboard until you have planned your animation.

Activity 1.4

You are going to create a short video about your favourite subject at school. This will be aimed at the parents, so you can tell them about what you enjoy doing at school.

When you create a storyboard for a video, make sure you describe what will happen in each frame. For example "Video of the outside of the school building, moving to the main entrance".

Plan your video using a storyboard. Make sure you include at least three frames.

Skill 2

Key term

Import: to move data into a computer program.

Creating source material for an animation

Animations can use images you have made on a computer. You can sometimes create these in the animation software itself, or you can create separate images and then **import** them into the software.

It is important to remember that every image, or part of an image, that you want to move independently needs to be a separate image. For example if you are creating a robot, and you want it to wave, then the arm needs to be separate from the rest of the robot. This lets you make the arm move without the rest of the robot moving.

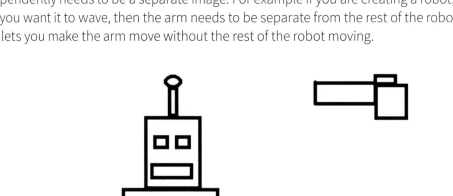

You can use any image creation software to create the images, just make sure they are saved as separate images, with suitable names, in a folder, and as suitable file types (for example .bmp files). There are lots of different file types you can use.

When you are creating your source material you need to think about the following questions:

- Which elements do you want to move independently?
- How large are the images? Are they in **proportion** to each other?
- How complex are the images? Sometimes simpler can be better.
- What colour are the images? Do they have one colour, or lots of colours? How do these colours work together? Are the colours appropriate?

If you do not want to create your own images, you can use pre-existing images, for example from other people or that you download from the internet. You may want to use these as they are, or **edit** them to make them more appropriate for your animation.

Creating source material for a video

A video can be made of lots of short videos that you put together. This source material could be pre-existing videos, for example ones you get from other people, or from the internet. You can also create your own videos using a video camera, a webcam or the camera in a mobile phone. These recordings are called **footage**.

If you are creating videos with other people in, you need to ask their permission first. Some people may not want to be in a video so you will not be able to use them. You need to respect this.

Creating your own videos depends on the hardware you use (the camera). Common tools you will need to make use of include the following:

Focus

A camera can **focus** on one element such as the part that is sharp and clearly visible. The other parts may be out of focus, or blurry. Using focus lets you make it clear which element your audience should be looking at.

> **Key terms**
>
> **Proportion:** how different things or parts relate to each other in number or size.
>
> **Edit:** to change something. For example you could change what some text says or make an image brighter.

> **Tip**
>
> Always check the copyright restrictions when using someone else's work. You may not be allowed to use or edit their images or videos.

> **Key terms**
>
> **Footage:** a recording of images in a video.
>
> **Focus:** when taking a video or photo, the area in focus is clear and precise. The rest of the image may be blurry.

Tip

You will need to practise using a camera before taking your videos. Try moving the camera at different speeds. The slower you move, the clearer the image. Moving it faster can make elements blur (which can represent speed).

Key term

Zoom: zooming in gets you closer to an image and enlarges it. Zooming out moves you away from the image and makes it smaller.

Tip

Your teacher will show you how to transfer the files from your hardware device.

Zoom

A camera may have a **zoom** button that lets you zoom in and out. Zooming in lets you get closer to the image and makes the element you are looking at larger. Zooming out makes the element smaller, and you get more of the surroundings in the image.

Here is an original image (on the left) that has then been zoomed in on (on the right) to give more detail on some of the buildings.

When you have recorded your videos, you need to transfer them onto your computer. How you do this will depend on the hardware you used to record them.

1. The device may have an SD (Secure Digital) card in. You will need to remove this, put it in your computer and then copy the files.

2. You may have a cable that you plug into the camera and your computer. You will then be able to access the camera's files on your computer to copy them across.

3. The device may have internet access which means you can attach your images to an email and send them to yourself.

Whichever method you use, you will need to create a folder on your computer to store the videos in. Make sure you give each video an appropriate name, so you know what it includes.

Panning

Panning is when you move the camera from one place to another in a slow, steady movement. For example, the camera starts off pointing to the right and is gradually turned towards the left so as to bring a person into the shot.

Activity 2.1

Create the individual images you need for your animation about your hobbies (that you planned in **Activities 1.1**, **1.2** and **1.3**).

Create a folder to store your images.

Save each image with an appropriate name.

Make sure every element you want to animate independently is a separate image.

Activity 2.2

Create the individual videos you need for your video about your favourite subject.

Create a folder to store your videos.

Transfer the videos to your computer and save each video with an appropriate name.

Skill 3

Creating an animation

An animation uses a **timeline** and frames. The timeline is a series of boxes, each one is a frame, or a single image.

1	2	3	4	5	6	7	8	9	10	11	12	13	14	15	16	17	18

19	20	21	22	23	24	25

In this timeline there are 25 frames. Each frame can have a different image in it, or just a change from the previous frame. When the animation is run, the frames 1 to 25 appear one after the other, creating the animation.

Navigating Pencil2D

There are lots of different pieces of software you can use to create an animation. Some of these can be downloaded, some of them can be used online. In this module you will use a piece of 2D animation software named Pencil2D that you need to download to use. Your teacher will help you with this.

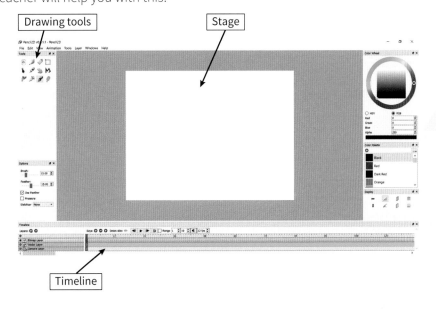

This is the **interface** for Pencil2D.

The **stage** is the area where the animation will take place. This is where you draw, or **insert** your images and make them move.

Drawing tools allow you to create shapes, change colours, add text, and so on.

In Pencil2D there are four layers. The bitmap layer is the one where you can use the drawing tools to create your images.

Creating a stop frame animation

If you take a notebook and draw a dot in the bottom right-hand corner, then on the next page change it slightly (move it, make it larger, or smaller), then again on the next page and keep repeating this. When you flick through all these pages it will look as if your image is moving. This is a basic stop frame animation.

This is the type of animation you can create in Pencil2D. Each frame in the timeline is one of the pages in the book.

Drawing in a frame

You can draw a shape, or image, in the first frame by first clicking on the paintbrush. After choosing your colour on the right-hand side, you can then hold your left mouse button to draw on the stage.

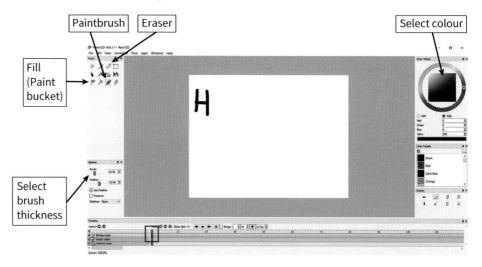

Adding new frames

You can create a new blank frame by clicking on the first **+** button next to the word 'Keys'. This will give you a completely empty stage. Use this to delete everything you had before and draw something new.

To create a **duplicate** frame (it will be identical to the previous one), you need to click on the second **+** button. You would use this to change your previous image (for example move it or add something to it).

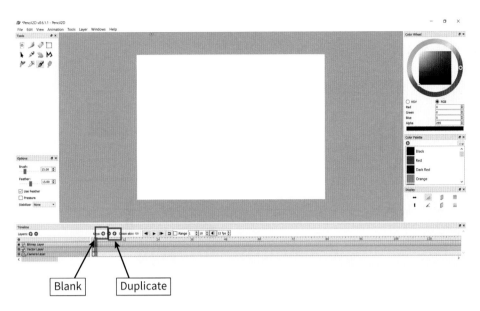

Blank | Duplicate

Deleting a frame

To delete a frame, you need to select the frame by clicking on the box above the layers.

You would then click on the − button to remove that frame.

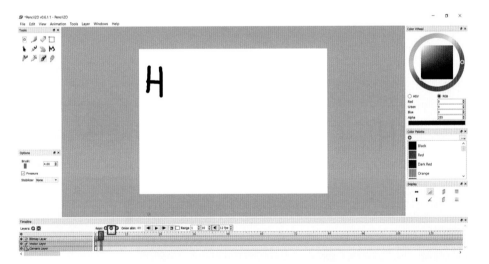

Playing your animation

To watch your animation, click on the **Play** button.

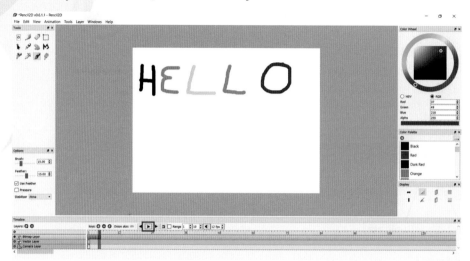

Changing the speed of your animation

The speed the animation runs at is called the **frames per second** or fps. The higher the fps, the faster the animation will run. If you reduce the fps, then each frame will stay on screen longer.

You can change the fps by entering a different number in the fps box.

Moving images

To move an image you need to use the select tool to highlight the part(s) you want to move. You would then use the arrow to move the image.

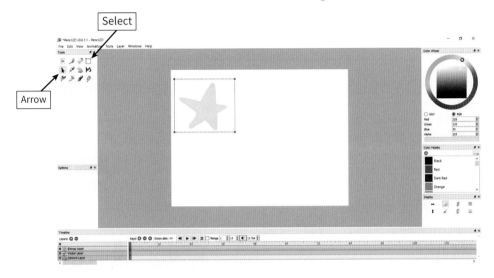

Using pre-existing images

You can import images that you have already made into your animation.

Each new image should have its own layer. This keeps them separate, and stops you from drawing over one of the images (for example rubbing out part of an image you didn't mean to).

To create a new layer, you need to click on the 'Layer +' symbol and select either Bitmap or Vector layer, depending which your image is.

A **bitmap** image is made of **pixels**. Each pixel is one small square that has one colour. These pixels make up the image. If you take a photo with a camera this will be a bitmap image. Paint software will usually create bitmap files. If you zoom in on a bitmap image

Key terms

Bitmap: an image stored as individual squares (pixels) that each have one colour.

Pixel: a single square of one colour in a bitmap image.

Key terms

Pixelating: when a bitmap image is enlarged, each pixel gets larger and the image goes blurry.

Vector: an image stored as coordinates and calculations.

then it will go blurry, this is called **pixelating**. A bitmap image may be a .bmp, .jpeg, .gif, .png or .tiff file.

A **vector** image is stored as coordinates and instructions. These instructions allow the image to be redrawn every time you open it, or make it larger or smaller. Vector images are only made using computers. A vector image may be an .eps, .psd, or .ai file.

Most of the images you will work with are likely to be bitmap images.

Make sure you give your new layer an appropriate name that describes the image.

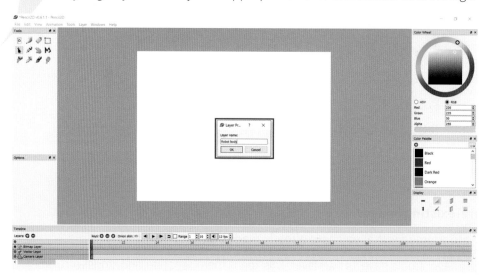

To import an image, you first need to make sure you have clicked on the layer you want the image inserting into. Then you need to click on **File**, 'Import' and then 'Image'.

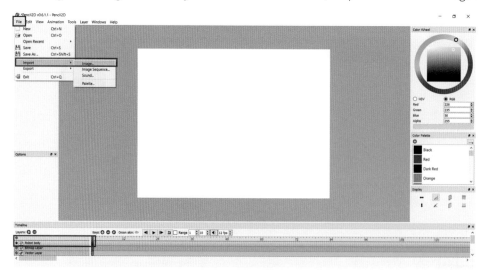

You can now animate, and change, your image.

Activity 3.1

Create a new Pencil2D file.

Create an animation that makes your name appear one letter at a time. Put each letter in a new frame.

Activity 3.2

Extend your animation from **Activity 3.1**.

Add other elements, for example stars that appear when your name has been fully written.

Activity 3.3

Create another new Pencil2D file.

Create an animation that makes a flower grow. Start the flower with just a small green dot, then in each frame make the flower stem taller, adding leaves, petals, and so on.

Activity 3.4

Create another new Pencil2D file.

Create an animation that moves a shape from one side of the screen to the other.

Activity 3.5

Draw two images in separate software and save them as bitmap files. For example you might draw a flower and a tree.

Create a new Pencil2D file.

Import each image into its own (appropriately named) layer.

Make your images move across the screen.

Activity 3.6

Create a new Pencil2D file.

Create your planned animation about your hobbies using the content created for **Activity 2.1**.

Did you know?

Some animation software will let you set the start position of a shape, the end position, and the number of frames you want it to take to move from the start to end positions. This is called adding a **tween**. It makes the movement smooth by calculating where the shape will be at each point.

Tip

Move the shape a small amount in each frame. The smaller the movements (and the more frames), the smoother the animation will be.

Key term

Tween: a computer animation tool that calculates the movements to make them smooth.

Tip

Remember to save your files!

Creating a new video

There are lots of different pieces of software that you can use to create a video. One example that you will use in this module is Adobe Spark. Other software includes Windows Photos.

A video can be created by combining lots of shorter individual videos, text, non-moving images, and sound. The order of these can be changed to create the final product. Each of these items is called a frame.

Transitions are motion effects that can be inserted between different individual video clips to make the change from one clip to another more interesting. Effects can also be added to the clips to change their appearance, such as changing the colours or adding a 'crackle' effect to make the clip look like an old fashioned movie.

Adobe Spark runs online. You will need to set up an account but your teacher will help you do this.

You will need to experiment with some alternative video editing software to explore and customise transitions and effects, as Adobe Spark does not support these features.

To use Adobe Spark when you create a new video, you will need to click on the **+** button.

You will then need to scroll down to the very bottom of the screen and click on 'Create a video'.

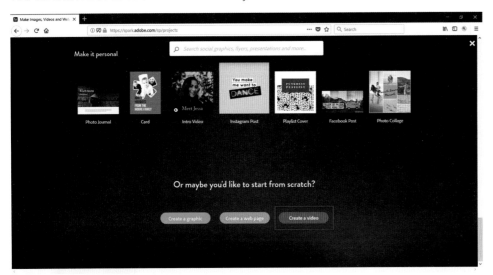

You should enter a title for your video and click on 'Next'.

Every great story starts somewhere

Tell us about your idea or title, you can always change it later.

My hobbies

Clicking on 'Start from scratch' will create a new, blank video.

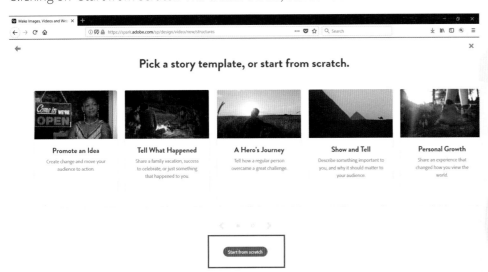

Adding elements to the video

To add a new frame you will need to click on the **+**. There will be four options for you to add to the frame: a video, some text, a photo or an icon.

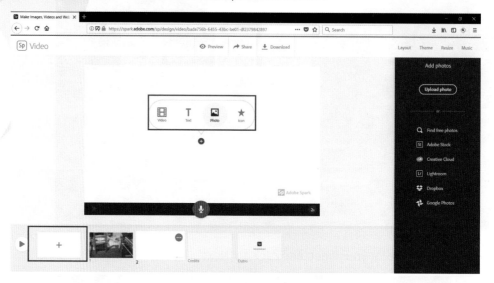

Video

When you click on **Video** you will then need to navigate to the folder where your video is stored and select it to upload. You then click on 'Open'.

You can move the bar to set which part of the video clip you want. The first circle shows where the clip will start, the second is where it will end. Only this part of the clip will be uploaded.

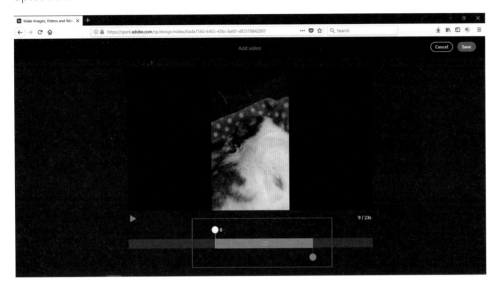

The video will then upload. This may take a while (depending on the size of your video) so be patient. Then click the **Save** button in the top corner.

To zoom in on the image, click on either the pencil icon or the three dots in the top right hand corner of the screen. If you click on the pencil icon then the three dots will appear.

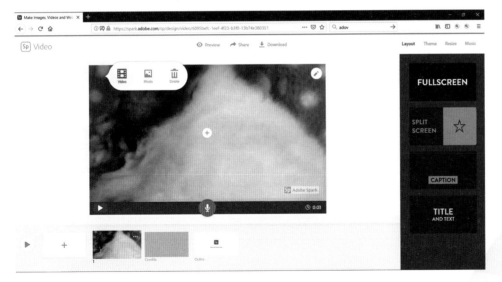

Click on the magnifying glass to select zoom.

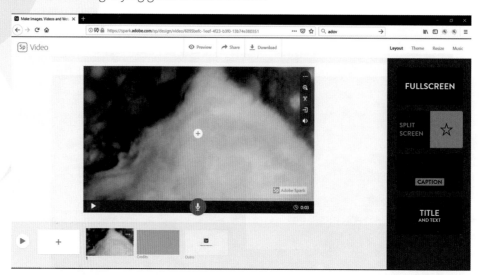

Click on the + magnifying glass to zoom in on the image, and the - magnifying glass to zoom out.

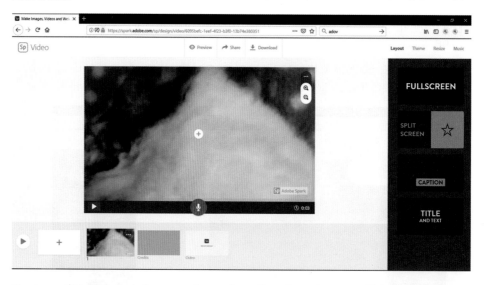

To stop editing, just click somewhere else other than the magnifying glass icons.

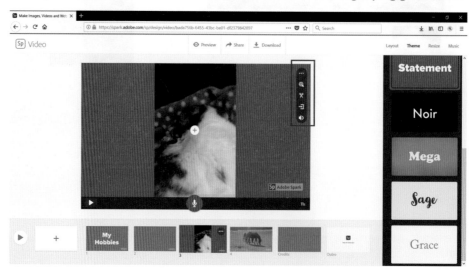

Image

When you click on **Image**, you will need to click on 'Upload photo' then select the image to upload.

Text

When you click on **Text**, a box will appear for you to enter your text in.

You have limited choices in fonts and colours unless you have the professional version of the software. It does have pre-set themes that you can choose from, however. This is where you will choose what font, colours and so on, to use in your video.

When you click on **Theme** you can choose one of the options to change the background of your video and the font format.

You can also add text to a slide with a video, or image, on.

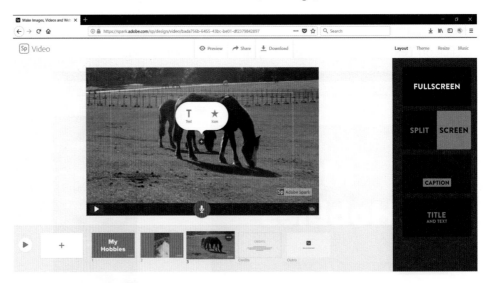

After you have clicked on the video, or image, you will need to click on the **+** button in the centre of the frame, then choose 'Text'.

Deleting

You may have added some content, or a frame, that you want to delete. To delete the frame, you will need to click on it and then the three dots in the corner. Click 'Delete' to remove it.

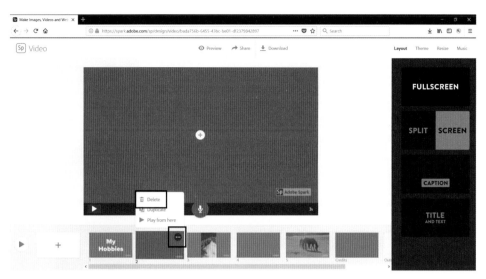

Reordering

You can change the order of the frames, by using the left mouse button to drag them to a new position.

Playing and downloading your video

When you want to watch your video you will need to click on the **Preview** button. When you are happy with your video, click on **Download** to watch it using your computer.

Once you have downloaded your video you will need to watch it using a **media player**. This is a piece of software that lets you watch videos on your computer, for example Windows Media Player. This software can read lots of different file types and play them on your computer.

Key terms

Preview: to watch something before it has been finished.

Download: to copy data from a computer to your computer using the internet.

Media player: a piece of software that allows you to watch videos on a computer.

Skill 5

Add a soundtrack or narration to your animation or video

You can add extra sound files to your animation or video so they play at the same time. A **narration** is a commentary, where you (or someone else) talks while images appear on the screen. A **soundtrack** is music that you add to the video or animation that plays in the background.

Key terms

Narration: the audio commentary that can be heard while images are shown.

Soundtrack: music that can be heard while images are shown.

If you want to use a song, or someone else's music, then you need to check if it is copyrighted and whether you are allowed to use it. You can usually use music for your own purposes, but if you are going to upload it to a website then you need to have permission. The easiest way is to make your own music.

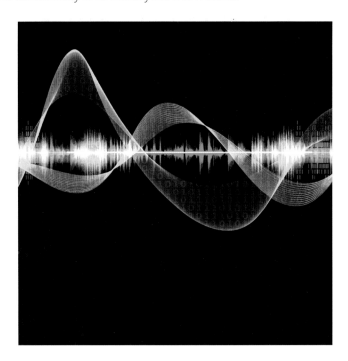

Adding sound to animation

Pencil2D has a sound layer. To add the sound layer, click on the **Layer +** button and choose **New Sound Layer**. Make sure you give it an appropriate name.

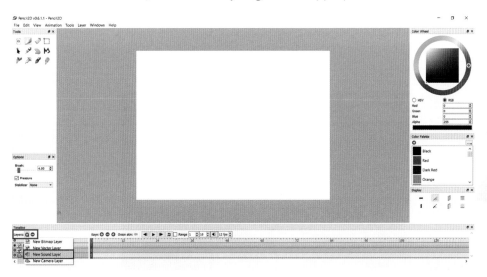

You will then need to click on your new sound layer, then the header of the frame where you want to add the sound file to. After you click on **Insert Blank Frame** you will need to choose your sound file from your documents.

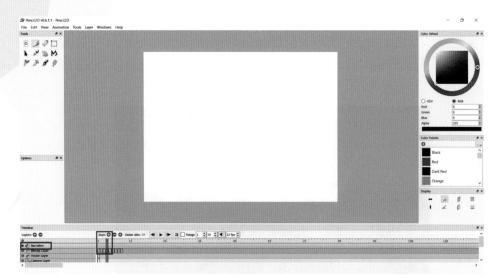

Your sound will appear in the layer, starting on the frame you selected. You cannot change the length of the sound file in Pencil2D. If you only want part of the sound file, then you need to edit this before you insert the sound file. The challenge task later in this module shows you how to do this.

If you want to add narration then you will need to create this using other software, for example Microsoft Sound Recorder, Audacity, or using your mobile phone. The file you create will need to be saved as either a .mp3 or .wav file to be inserted into Pencil2D.

Adding narration to a video

When you create a frame in Adobe Spark, you will see a microphone button. If you click on this your computer will ask if you want to give permission to Adobe Spark to access your microphone.

To record the sound, you will need to hold your left mouse button down on the microphone button and speak into your microphone. This sound will now be stored on the frame you selected.

To add pre-recorded sound, or sound already within Adobe Spark, click on the **Music** menu.

You will first need to click on the frame that you want the sound to appear on, then select one of the sounds from the menu, or click on 'Add my music' to choose a file you have already saved.

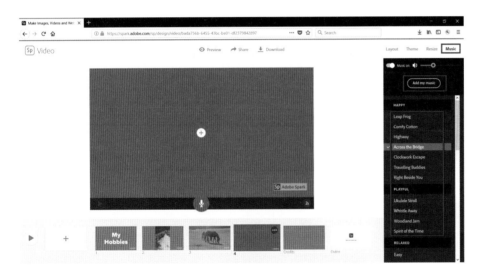

Activity 5.1

Add a soundtrack to your animation about your hobbies from **Activity 3.5**.

Activity 5.2

Add a narration to your video about your favourite subject from **Activity 3.4**.

Activity 5.3

Add a soundtrack, or sound effect to part of your video about your favourite subject from **Activity 3.4**.

Meeting the needs of a specific audience

Your audience may consist of one person or multiple people who are going to view your video. You may have one specific person or you may have a range of people, for example children aged between 10 and 13. Or, it could be anyone!

When planning your video or animation, you need to make sure it is suitable for your audience. After making it, you will need to explain how you made sure it was appropriate.

The table has some ideas on how you can do this, but they don't all apply in every scenario.

Audience	Appropriate features
Young children	Use bright colours
	Use short/simple words
	Use images more than text
	Use cartoon/fun images
	Use informal language
Adults	Use more text
	Use more sophisticated language/words
	Use formal language
	Use images to support the text (not instead of text)
Older children	Use a range of colours
	Informal or formal, depending on your topic
	Use images to support and enhance text

Activity 6.1

Who was the intended audience for your animation about your hobbies?

_____

How did you make sure the animation was appropriate for the audience? Use the headings below to help you write your answer.

Images:

_____

_____

Text:

_____

_____

Sound:

_____

_____

Activity 6.2

Who was the intended audience for your video about your favourite subject?

_____

How did you make sure the video was appropriate for the audience? Use the headings below to help you write your answer.

Images:

_____

_____

Text:

_____

_____

Sound:

_____

_____

Scenario

Advertising a product

You have been asked to create a short advert for a new healthy chocolate bar named 'Fizzfizz'.

Your advert should be either an animation or a video. It should last between 10 and 30 seconds and should be aimed at children aged between 10 and 15 years old.

Activity 1

Plan an animation or video to advertise Fizzfizz using a storyboard.

Activity 2

Create and/or gather the individual content items you will need for the animation or video you have planned.

Make sure you:

- create a suitable folder to store them in
- give each file an appropriate name
- store each piece of content as an appropriate file type.

Activity 3

Create your animation or video.

Activity 4

Add a soundtrack and/or narration to your video.

Activity 5

Write a short report explaining how you made sure your animation or video was appropriate for the intended audience.

Challenge

Audacity is a piece of software that lets you create and edit sound files. There are lots of other pieces of software that will also let you do this, for example Adobe Audition, or ocenaudio.

Opening a file

When you have opened the software, click on **File** and then **Open** to select the sound file you want to change.

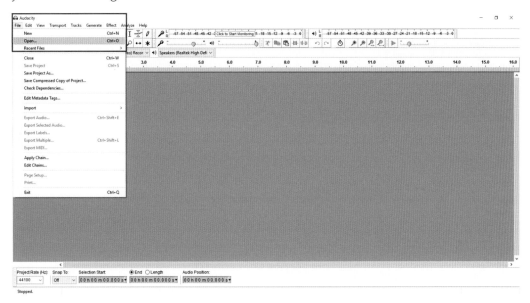

You can then choose the file and select it to open.

Recording sound

To create your own sound, or add sound to a pre-existing file, click on the red record button and then speak into the microphone.

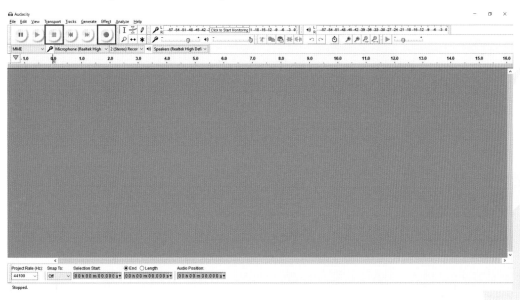

To stop recording you will need to click on the yellow stop button.

Playing sound

To play back the sound, first click on the selection tool, and then where you want to start playing from. Click on the **Play** button to listen to your sound file.

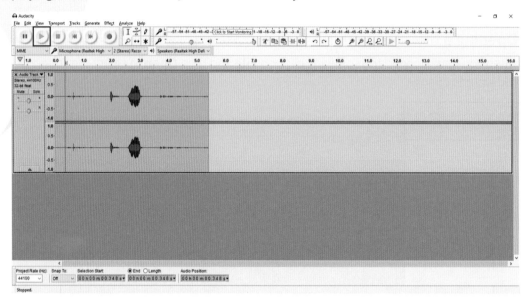

Selecting sound

The 'Selection' tool lets you highlight sections of sound. You can then copy, cut, and delete this section by clicking on **Edit** and then choosing what you want to do.

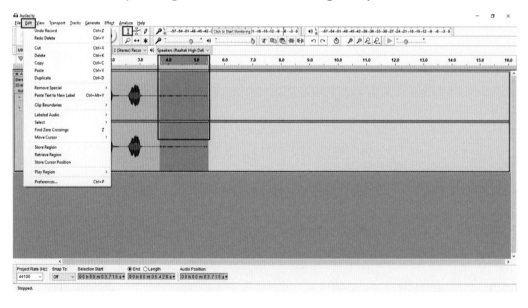

Adding effects

Audacity has built-in effects that you can add to your sound file, for example fade in, fade out, and so on. To add an effect, use the 'Selection' tool to highlight the area of the sound wave you want the effect applied to. Then click on 'Effect' from the top menu and choose the effect you want.

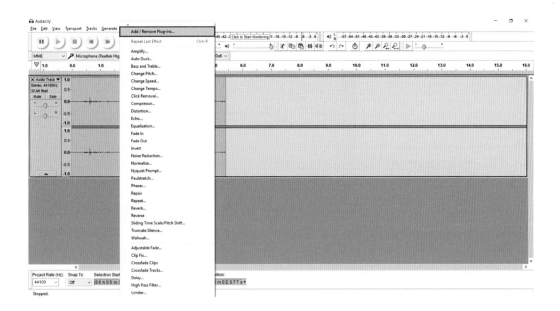

Saving the sound

If you are editing a file you already had, make sure you save it under a different name, otherwise you will overwrite the original.

To save the file, click on **File**, then 'Save'.

Exporting the sound

You may need the sound file to be in a specific format, for example .mp3.

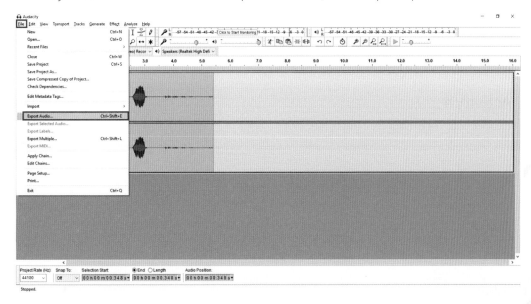

When you are happy with your sound file, click on **File** and then 'Export Audio'.

Choose the appropriate folder for your file, and give it a suitable filename. From the drop-down box choose the file type you want to save it as.

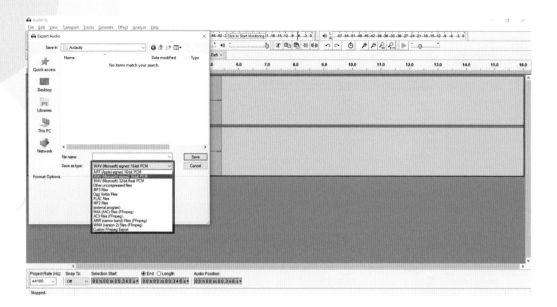

Activity 1

Create a new narrative for your video about your favourite subject using Audacity.

Activity 2

Edit your recording, deleting parts you do not want.

Activity 3

Add effects to your recording, for example fading in at the start, and fading out at the end.

Activity 4

Export your recording as a .mp3 file.

Final project – Join our school!

You have been asked to create a short advert for potential new students visiting your school.

Your advert should be either an animation or a video. It should last between 10 and 40 seconds and should be aimed at children aged between 9 and 15 years old. It needs to tell them about your school, subjects, and so on.

Activity 1

Plan an animation or video to advertise your school using a storyboard.

Activity 2

Create and/or gather the individual content items you will need for the animation or video you have planned.

Make sure you:

- create a suitable folder to store them in
- give each file an appropriate name
- store each piece of content as an appropriate file type.

Activity 3

Create your animation or video.

Activity 4

Use Audacity to create a narrative and/or soundtrack for your video or animation.

Activity 5

Add your narrative and/or soundtrack to your video or animation.

Activity 6

Write a short report explaining how you made sure your animation or video was appropriate for the intended audience.

> **Tip**
>
> You will need to submit your work for marking. To do this make sure your video or animation is on a USB memory stick or a disk, and that all the files (e.g. including soundtracks) are copied correctly.

Reflection

1 Explain when it is best to use animation instead of video.

_____

_____

_____

_____

2 Explain why it is important to get permission before taking photos or videos of other people.

_____

_____

_____

_____

3 Explain what copyright is and why it is important it is not broken.

_____

_____

_____

_____

4 Explain why it is important that your product is suitable for its intended audience.

_____

_____

_____

_____